"The Beveres are some of the most purehearted people I know. Their choice to push through and remain obedient to God's instruction for this book in such unprecedented times speaks greatly to their genuine desire to help and transform lives. *I AM: Find Your Identity. Claim Your Freedom. Embrace the Adventure.,* is a game changer! Sons & Daughters challenges us to find the beauty in the unknown and to consistently seek God's plan and purpose as we mature in our relationship with him. Get ready for an honest, challenging, and exhilarating ride as you journey through this read and begin unraveling and letting go of what was never meant so you may walk in total freedom and victory!"

Heather Lindsey, speaker, author, and founder of Pinky Promise Movement

"*I AM* is more than a collection of positive declarations; it's an all-out war against the lies that have kept a generation confined and disillusioned. If you're ready to become who God says you are, then *I AM* will equip you with the truth to get started!"

Henry and Alex Seeley, senior pastors of The Belonging Co

"Most of the time what we speak comes from what we believe. In Sons & Daughters' new book *I AM*, we get strong biblical truth to fill our minds and emotions. Believing truth renews our thoughts and changes how we speak about ourselves and others."

Brian and Jenn Johnson, worship leaders and copresidents of Bethel Music

I AM

I AM

FIND YOUR **IDENTITY**.

CLAIM YOUR **FREEDOM**.

EMBRACE THE **ADVENTURE**.

SONS & DAUGHTERS

Revell

a division of Baker Publishing Group
Grand Rapids, Michigan

Published by Revell
a division of Baker Publishing Group
PO Box 6287, Grand Rapids, MI 49516-6287
www.revellbooks.com

Printed in the United States of America

Library of Congress Cataloging-in-Publication Data
Names: Sons & Daughters (Colorado Springs, Colo.), author.
Title: I am : find your identity. claim your freedom. embrace the adventure. / Sons & Daughters.
Description: Grand Rapids, Michigan : Revell, a division of Baker Publishing Group, [2021]
Identifiers: LCCN 2021003896 | ISBN 9780800737689 (paperback) | ISBN 9781493431823 (ebook)
Subjects: LCSH: Young adults—Religious life. | Self-actualization (Psychology)—Religious aspects—Christianity.
Classification: LCC BV4529.2 .S67 2021 | DDC 248.8/4—dc23
LC record available at https://lccn.loc.gov/2021003896

In keeping with biblical principles of creation stewardship, Baker Publishing Group advocates the responsible use of our natural resources. As a member of the Green Press Initiative, our company uses recycled paper when possible. The text paper of this book is composed in part of post-consumer waste.

green press INITIATIVE

21 22 23 24 25 26 27   7 6 5 4 3 2 1

To the sons and daughters who've paved the way,
the ones embracing the adventure today,
and those who will lead one day.

CONTENTS

THE
ADVENTURE

HAVE YOU EVER FOUND YOURSELF THINKING, *There must be more to life than this, right?* It's an uncomfortable thought and one that seems to creep in at the most unexpected and inopportune times. It calls into question our choices, our plans, our values, and some of our basic assumptions about life. Most of us have put so much time and effort into succeeding that we find existential questions like that one not only inconvenient but intimidating. And yet no matter how often we push it down and just carry on with life as normal, the question still seems to resurface at regular intervals.

What if that question isn't just a dreamy distraction from real life? What if it's more than unrealistic idealism? What if God has a future for you that goes far beyond your current reality and your own ideas of who you are and what you can achieve?

The truth is, God didn't create you to live a life of predictable, boring, self-centered comfort. He didn't make you content to be like everyone else. He didn't design you to fit a mold, match a pattern, or fill a role. God created you unique, one of a kind, with a future that is as individual as you are. So when the thought that *there must be more to life than this* arises, there's a good chance God himself is trying to get your attention.

When you were brought into God's family, you became his son or daughter. That identity change is nothing short of revolutionary. At least, it should be. But the pressures of responsibilities and the monotony of the daily grind have a way of shifting our eyes away from who we are to focusing us, slave-like, on what we must do. In his book *Walden*, philosopher Henry Thoreau famously observed that "the mass of men live lives of quiet desperation." But that is not your calling. That is not your destiny. And while we hope it's not your current reality, if it is, we are here to offer hope.

GOD CREATED YOU UNIQUE, ONE OF A KIND, WITH A FUTURE THAT IS AS INDIVIDUAL AS YOU ARE.

We are passionate about helping people understand their identity, live in the freedom and joy that following God's calling brings, and become leaders in their sphere of influence.

We want you to see yourself the way God sees you. Only from that will you grow in the confidence and the strength to really *live* this adventure that we call life. The deep yearnings inside of you—the desires to be loved, to have a purpose, to succeed, to know God, to impact others—were put there by God, not to taunt you but to encourage you to step into the unknown and experience fully the life God created for you.

Are you listening to that voice? Are you up for the adventure? It won't be easy. Stepping out and exploring the unknown is risky. There will be some fears to face and a few giants to defeat. But not only is the destination worth the journey, the journey itself is priceless. You were created for adventure. You were built to yearn for more than the predictable, self-centered life you see around you. And God himself is calling you to step into a future that holds more than you can imagine.

MIDDLE SCHOOL REDUX

Remember middle school? Do you even *want* to remember it? If you're like a lot of us, you've probably spent the last decade or two trying to forget that stage. You might still wake up in a cold sweat every once in a while, remembering some awkward moment that doesn't matter anymore . . . but somehow still does.

GOD HIMSELF IS CALLING YOU TO STEP INTO A FUTURE THAT HOLDS MORE THAN YOU CAN IMAGINE.

It's funny how middle school only lasts a few years, but for many of us, they are some of the most awkward, change-filled years of our lives. Hormones. Bullying. Braces. Group projects. Peer drama. Romance and betrayal. Plans for the future and doubts about the future and then more plans for the future.

This period of life is often called coming of age, and it's the subject of countless movies and books. Why? Because there is something fascinating about how children morph into adults, or at least, into mini adults. It is a period of rapid growth, of new understanding, of self-awareness, of firsts, of developing talents and discovering passions, of self-confidence mixed with self-doubt, of intense emotions, of questioning everyone and everything.

More likely than not, middle school has long since disappeared from your rearview mirror. But you've probably noticed something: that strange mix of growth and chaos we call middle school was really a preview of every season of change you'll ever go through. Coming of age is really just the beginning of the rest of your life, and life is not always as easy or clear-cut as you might like it to be. It has ups and downs, twists and turns, laughter and tears. You never outgrow doubts and questions. You never leave behind growth and dreams.

Being a young adult, in particular, can feel like middle school all over again, except you probably don't have braces and the stakes are a lot higher. Oh, and it doesn't end in a few years. That isn't meant to be depressing—it's actually comforting, in a twisted way, because it means that a certain level of doubt or fear, of anxiety or questioning or panic, is *normal*.

If you've ever felt overwhelmed by the uncertainty of the future, that's normal.

If you've ever felt intimidated by the size of the decisions you are facing, that's normal.

If you've ever felt disillusioned by the path you thought you were meant to take, that's normal.

If you've ever questioned anything and everything, up to and including God, that's normal.

If you've ever felt like there are more changes than constants, that's normal.

If you've ever felt alone, depressed, confused, scared, and angry, and simultaneously excited, energized, passionate, and creative, that's normal.

If you're constantly dreaming but not really sure how to make those dreams happen, that's normal.

If you sometimes feel like you're not moving forward fast enough, or even that life is leaving you behind, that's normal.

If you're searching for meaning, identity, and value, that's normal.

IT'S NORMAL TO FEEL LIKE A MESS IN MOTION AND A WORK IN PROGRESS.

By *normal* we don't mean things will stay this way. Rather, we mean you aren't a bad person or a lost soul or a hopeless mess just because you don't have your entire life in order within ten years of finishing high school. It's normal to feel like a mess in motion and a work in progress. It's normal to struggle with deep questions, deep emotions, and deep passions from time to time. It's normal to experience change and for that change to throw things into disarray for a while.

Simply put, welcome to the rest of your life. It's a crazy life, but it's your life. You get to live it; no one else. You get to experience firsts. You get to choose the paths you take. You get to learn and grow along the way. You get to dream big and pursue those dreams. You get to build friendships and family connections that stand the test of time. And you get to experience each day, no matter what that day brings.

It's this sense of destiny mixed with chaos that motivated us to begin Sons & Daughters, actually. And it's the reason we've written this book. We are passionate about helping people embrace the adventure that is life, with all its ups and downs and crazy paradoxes.

We'd like to say right up front that the purpose of this book is not to tell you how to live your life. That's up to God and you.

However, we would like to show you what the Bible says about how to figure out how to live that life.

That's a lot of *hows* and *tos* all strung together in one sentence. But notice the difference. We aren't telling you how to live, but rather how to figure out life for yourself. Your path won't be exactly the same as anyone else's. The answers you give to some of life's questions will be different from those around you. That's okay. In fact, it's beautiful. You were never meant to be a clone.

But you also aren't alone in this journey of life. You don't have to figure everything out unaided. There are some foundational truths in the Bible that will help you navigate through what life throws at you. So while it's your life, we have no intention of telling you what your journey must look like or which way to go at each fork in the road. We are here to share a few truths that will help you along the way. These are things that have shaped us profoundly in our individual journeys, and we believe they will transform yours as well.

So, let's get started.

WHO I AM In this book we'd like to share seven truths about *who* God sees when he looks at you. We call them our "I Am" statements. They are foundational beliefs—based on God's revelation of himself in the Bible—that will help you find meaning and purpose throughout your life. Here's the list, which we'll unpack in the next few chapters:

1. I AM HOLY.
2. I AM RIGHTEOUS.
3. I AM LOVED.
4. I AM SECURE.
5. I AM CONFIDENT.
6. I AM CREATIVE.
7. I AM CALLED.

These are biblical truths, but they are also deeply personal, experiential ones. So throughout the rest of this book, we have included contributions that convey how God's love, demonstrated in these statements, has transformed the lives of fellow sons and daughters who have been impacted by these truths.

These are truths we hope you will come back to time and time again, especially in times of change or growth or loss. You won't outgrow them, and you can never fully master them, because even though they look simple, they have deep ramifications across all areas of life. Instead, we hope you explore them, sit with them, and live them out. That you return to them when life gets crazy. That you let them shape you and then reshape you as you gain more experience in life.

That will look different for each of us, and it will look different from season to season. In every stage, every change, and every challenge, knowing the truth you stand upon is essential. Why? Because when things around you are shaking, you need something to hold on to.

WHEN THINGS AROUND YOU ARE SHAKING, YOU NEED SOMETHING TO HOLD ON TO.

Take a look at the following list, presented in no particular order. Are you going through any of these right now? Or do you think you might experience them in the near future?

Graduating high school

Graduating college

Moving into your own apartment or home

Getting a job

Quitting a job

Getting a better job

Getting fired

Buying a home

Finding a girlfriend or boyfriend

Breaking up with your boyfriend or girlfriend

Getting married

Having a kid

Starting a business

Going back to school

Changing careers

Losing a loved one

Moving across the country

Learning to be a better spouse

Learning to be a better parent

The list could go on forever, but here's the point. The instability and changeability of life are real, but that doesn't mean changes or challenges have to derail you. Instead, the truths you hold at the core of your belief system will help you adapt and grow through each stage.

Holding on to truth does not mean stubbornly refusing to change your mind about anything though. Don't confuse "core beliefs" and "narrow worldviews." While your core beliefs should be based on the Bible and will remain relatively unchanged, who is to say that every opinion you now hold is perfectly accurate and will never need improvement or adjustment as you grow? That's a rhetorical question, by the way. You can be sure you *aren't* totally right about everything—and that's okay.

Actually, valuing and pursuing truth will lead you to change your mind about some things on a regular basis as you grow and learn. If you believe exactly the same thing in ten years that you do now, that's a problem. If anything, you should be skeptical of people who have it all figured out—whether that's money, theology, marriage, or any other area—especially if they haven't faced too many challenges in life yet. We all must recognize that our knowledge is "partial and incomplete," as Paul wrote to the Corinthians (1 Cor. 13:12 NLT).

Hopefully knowing you can change your mind from time to time takes some of the pressure off. Think of these seven statements as starting points, realizing that there are an infinite number of ways to live them out. Then trust yourself—and, much more importantly, trust God at work in you—to face even the most unexpected moments with wisdom and peace.

PERSPECTIVES

SEVEN MILES DOESN'T SEEM FAR when you're driving a car. It takes maybe six or seven minutes on a freeway. Most of us wouldn't think twice about driving that far to pick up our favorite Chinese takeout or to drop off a friend at her house. We might drive two or three times that far on our daily work commute, so seven miles is not really a big deal.

Until you find yourself seven miles *straight up*. That works out to an altitude of thirty-seven thousand feet, a normal cruising height for commercial jetliners. If you think back to the last time you sat in the window seat of a jet, watching the ground fall away and familiar landmarks turn into toys, you know that gazing down from seven miles up can give you a whole new perspective. The obligatory airplane wing pictures all over Instagram are proof of that.

Seeing the earth from above reminds you how big the world is and how small you are. That perspective can make you feel tiny.

Even insignificant. You are one person, in one town, in one country, on one continent, on one planet, in one solar system, in one galaxy, in one random place in an infinitely expanding universe.

Flying through the sky in a hollow metal tube is a modern phenomenon, but contemplating human significance is as ancient as humanity itself. Throughout history, poets and philosophers, historians and artists, authors and monks have asked:

Who are we?

Why are we here?

Do we matter?

Do we have a purpose?

As humans, we have a deep need to find meaning in life. Something inside of us pushes us to seek a motive behind our existence. We don't want to just live and die anonymously—where's the significance in that? There has to be more to life than sleep, eat, work, repeat.

Maybe you've thought about this too. Maybe you've wondered if you are significant. If you are valuable. If you are unique. If you are gifted. Maybe you've asked whether you have a deeper purpose—some divine stamp, not just of approval but of destiny.

The Bible addresses these questions head-on. From start to end, it is a book not just about God but about how God intersects with humanity. It's the story of God creating us, loving us, and leading us. It is a revelation of our importance within his plan and his creation.

HUMAN DIGNITY AND WORTH ARE DIRECTLY RELATED TO THE GOD WHO MADE HUMANS.

Human dignity and worth are directly related to the God who made humans. His purpose for us, his love for us, and his value for us are what instill us with immeasurable, unshakable value. To find true identity or meaning in life apart from God is impossible because life comes from him. The more we understand God and the closer we come to him, the more we understand who we are and the infinite value we have.

That doesn't mean life is all about praying or reading the Bible or going to church or any other "spiritual" activity. The idea that being close to God can only take place in the context of some religious ritual or church building is an absolute myth. It reduces God to a religion box that we take out on Sundays or when we need to ask for something, only to be put back on a shelf once we're done.

Nothing could be further from the truth. *Every* activity, *every* pursuit, and *every* moment takes place in God's presence. Our entire lives are lived out under his gaze and for his pleasure. We can't run from him or hide from him; we can't scare him away or make him turn his back on us. He is always with us.

This means that the human quests for identity, value, and purpose are more mundane than we often think. Not mundane in the negative sense of boring or common but in the sense of being part of your day-to-day experience.

You won't discover the reason for your existence in a moment, a day, or even a season; such awareness is cultivated through a lifetime of discoveries. The most important things in life usually cannot be summed up in one or two simplistic sentences anyway. Your unique reason for existence cannot simply be reduced to a cute meme or pithy quote. It's multifaceted, like a beautifully cut diamond. And while that diamond probably still has a few (or many) rough edges, the one who created the gem isn't finished yet. He's still at work, shaping it into a thing of incomparable beauty.

That process of shaping and forming takes place through innumerable clarifying moments over the course of years. Some of those moments may be major, life-altering events that will stand

EVERY ACTIVITY, EVERY PURSUIT, AND EVERY MOMENT TAKES PLACE IN GOD'S PRESENCE.

out in your memory forever as key points in your personal history. Others will be seemingly trivial thoughts, conversations, and choices—tiny taps with the Designer's hammer that you may not even realize were significant at the time.

But through it all, God is leading you into the purpose he has created for you. He is stronger than your weakness, more patient than your stubbornness, wiser than your foolishness, and more faithful than your failures. He has a future, bold and beautiful, for you. Trust him in the journey to discover what that entails, and you will find the adventure you were created to pursue.

A SEVEN-MILE WALK As we saw earlier, being seven miles up gives you a good perspective of the ground below. The Bible talks about another seven-mile distance, however, that brought new perspective to a couple of unnamed men traveling from Jerusalem to a nearby town. Their experience has a lot to tell us about the "why" behind the concepts of calling, mission, and significance.

Maybe you've read this story before. It's often called "The Road to Emmaus," which sounds like a chapter in an epic fantasy novel, but actually just refers to the ancient stretch of road between Israel's capital city of Jerusalem and the neighboring village of Emmaus, about seven miles away.

The full story is found in Luke 24:13–35, and it takes place on the Sunday after Jesus's death. For context, just hours prior to this story, Mary Magdalene and a few other women had gone to Jesus's tomb and found it empty. As if that weren't bizarre enough, two angels calmly informed them that Jesus had risen from the dead. Peter and John didn't believe the women, so they went to check it out for themselves, probably expecting to mansplain the situation to the women, only to discover that what they had said was true. The tomb was empty. (See Luke 24:1–12.)

By early afternoon, rumors of Jesus's resurrection were spreading among his followers. No one knew what to believe. It was an understandable reaction, considering many of them had watched as Jesus's lifeless body was taken down from the cross by Roman soldiers and sealed in a tomb.

The death of Jesus and the breaking news of his possible resurrection, therefore, were the backdrop for the Road to Emmaus story. Luke starts by recounting how two men had set out for the small village. We don't know what business they had there, but it's clear that their minds were spinning from recent events. While they were walking and talking, a third man caught up to them and joined them on their road trip.

It was Jesus, of course. But the other two men didn't recognize him.

The miles and the hours passed in a dusty blur. As the trio walked toward Emmaus, Jesus took them through the Hebrew Scriptures, helping them understand more about the man they had thought was their Messiah . . . then thought had been lost forever . . . and now were beginning to think might be the Messiah after all. The men would later say that their hearts began to "burn within [them]" as Jesus unlocked the Scriptures (v. 32 ESV).

When they got to Emmaus, the men urged Jesus to stay with them so they could continue talking. He agreed, and they sat down for dinner. Jesus blessed the meal, broke the bread, and handed it to the men—then abruptly vanished from their sight. He always had a flair for the dramatic.

In that instant, the men realized they had been in the presence of Jesus. Their dinner was forgotten, along with whatever business they had in Emmaus. They ran the seven miles back to Jerusalem, found the other disciples, and began to tell them what had happened. While the group was frantically discussing the newest craziness in an already crazy day, Jesus appeared out of nowhere. Again with the drama.

Eventually the disciples regained their composure, but they couldn't contain their emotion. The rumors were true. Jesus was

EVERYTHING HAD CHANGED AFTER THIS SEVEN-MILE TRIP. CONFUSION TURNED TO CLARITY. FEAR BECAME CONFIDENCE. ANXIETY GAVE WAY TO PEACE.

back. He took a few minutes to encourage them and probably to have a bit of fun with them. Then he told them what was about to happen. He would be going back to heaven, but he would send the Holy Spirit to be with them, to lead them, and to teach them. Then he gave them a mission. They were to take what they knew about Jesus to a world that was far from God (Matt. 28:16–20 and Acts 1:8).

Notice the progression. First, they received a new perspective about *Jesus*: he had conquered death, he was truly the expected Messiah and Savior, and he would be with them through the Holy Spirit forever. Second, they received a new perspective about *themselves*: they had the power of God within them, they had been called for this time and this task, and their lives would make a difference in the world.

Everything had changed after this seven-mile trip. Confusion turned to clarity. Fear became confidence. Anxiety gave way to peace.

REGARDLESS OF WHAT DUSTY ROAD WE MIGHT BE TRAVELING RIGHT NOW, JESUS WANTS TO JOIN OUR ROAD TRIP.

THE WHY BEHIND OUR CALLING IS JESUS.

And perhaps most significantly of all, anonymity turned into calling.

Each of us needs a similar experience in our lives. Not so much the "it's a ghost, no it's just Jesus playing tricks again" experience, but the revelation that there is a calling on our lives. We need to know that regardless of what dusty road we might be traveling right now, Jesus wants to join our road trip. He wants to turn our anonymity and our inferiority and our mistakes and our passions and our dreams and our uniqueness into *calling*.

Remember where this transformation started though. It didn't start with the two men themselves. They didn't start their journey looking for Jesus or looking for calling—they just wanted to get to Emmaus by dinnertime. Throughout the story they were confused, hesitant, oblivious. They didn't recognize Jesus when he was literally staring them in the face. And yet, Jesus took the time to appear to them, to walk with them, to reveal himself to them.

Jesus took the initiative with these men, just as he does with us today. He cared about their understanding and their perspective enough to open their eyes, heal their hearts, and lay out their futures. When they saw Jesus, they understood themselves better. They realized there was a divine stamp upon their lives, and they were never the same again.

The rest is history. Jesus's disciples turned the world on its head. They went from region to region, from country to country, and from continent to continent telling people about Jesus. They started a movement that grew stronger with every generation. More than a religion, more than a set of doctrines, more than ritual or ceremony, Christianity is and always has been about Jesus.

Why are we called? Because Jesus gave his life for us, restored us, saved us, chose us, and commissioned us. Because Jesus values us and loves us. Because Jesus finds us and reveals himself to us. Because Jesus believes in us. Because Jesus will go with us to the ends of the earth and the end of time.

In other words, the why behind our calling is Jesus.

When you walk a few miles with Jesus, when you sit at a table with him, when he shows up in your day-to-day schedule and interrupts your agenda, something inevitably changes in you. When you see him for who he is, you see yourself for who you are. When you catch a glimpse of his greatness, his love, and his grace, you understand yourself and your purpose in life in a whole new light.

Jesus wants to meet you on your own road, wherever it is you're going. He wants to get to know you, to share in your life, and to open your eyes to who he is and what he has for you. What that looks like for you will be unique. That's the nature of relationships. No two are precisely alike; each is as unique as the people who form it. That's part of what makes your journey with Jesus so precious.

JESUS DOESN'T JUST WANT TO REVEAL HIMSELF TO YOU. HE ALSO WANTS TO REVEAL YOU TO YOU.

But he doesn't just want to reveal himself to you. He also wants to reveal *you* to you. He wants to help you see yourself in a new way. We tend to view ourselves through lenses that are fogged by wrong perceptions and scratched by hurtful experiences with others. Jesus wants to remove those false lenses and enable you to see yourself as a son or daughter of God, who is loved and accepted and chosen. In the next few chapters, we'll see what that looks like.

HOLY

ON AN AVERAGE WEEKDAY, if you listen to people talk around you, you'll probably hear the word *holy* a few times. It likely will have nothing to do with religion, of course. It will be linked to anything from animals ("holy cow") to bodily functions ("holy sh—") to an avocado dish ("holy guacamole") and everything in between.

On the other hand, if you hear the word *holy* on a Sunday, there's a good chance it will have to do with religion. It might refer to the fact that God is perfect or that we should live pure lives or that holiness means saying no to temptation or something similar.

The difference between those two meanings is drastic, isn't it? The first one is usually a spontaneous expression of emotion. The second one is solemn and serious. So which is right?

When used in the first context—i.e., the nonreligious one—the term *holy* often introduces a dramatic, emphatic statement of awe. People use it when they feel strongly about something (good or bad) and want to emphasize or magnify that feeling. Hold that thought—it's important.

The religious use of the word, on the other hand, usually refers to a lifestyle that is free from sin. We think of a holy person as someone who perfectly controls their impulses and urges, who abstains from wrong actions, and who lives without sin. We think of holiness as a spiritual goal: we should avoid sin and be committed to God. We think of a holy God as one who is perfect, who hates sin, and who is going to judge those who don't live up to his standard.

Here's the deal though. That religious definition is flawed. It reduces holiness to simply "not doing bad things," which doesn't even come close to the broad, beautiful idea of holiness in the Bible.

Unfortunately, this is the view many people have of holiness. They think God's endgame is to get us to behave. Because they know their lifestyle still has a few flaws, they react to the statement "You should be holy" the same way they react to someone saying, "You should go to the dentist." *Yes, I should. But I don't want to, because no matter how hard I try, I always get shamed. What I've done is never enough.*

Holiness was never meant to create guilt trips. (Dentistry wasn't either, in all fairness.) And if your reaction to the idea of holiness is one of guilt or shame or fear, chances are you haven't fully understood what the Bible means by the term. If your view of holiness has been reduced to *not* having sex outside of marriage, to *not* getting drunk, to *not* swearing, to *not* rebelling, to *not* doing

HOLINESS WAS NEVER MEANT TO CREATE GUILT TRIPS.

or saying or thinking sinful things, then you've missed the point altogether.

Ironically, holiness in the Bible might have more to do with the first definition above than the second. That is, it has more in common with awe than with moral behavior. Holiness in a biblical sense expresses how big, how awesome, and how unique something is. It is not about following a list of rules but about feeling a sense of amazement and respect for what is truly impressive.

That doesn't mean holiness is disconnected from sin, of course. It just means sin isn't the point. Good moral choices are not the sum total of holiness. Being on our best behavior is not the end goal. Those are some of the byproducts of holiness, as we'll see later, but they are not the focus.

So what *is* the focus of holiness? Awe. Wonder. Purity. Greatness. Worship. Value. Respect.

Without a doubt, we all need more "holy" in our lives. But that should not be interpreted to mean we should all feel more ashamed or more guilty or more afraid. Rather, we need to grow in awe, in wonder, in respect. First with regard to *God* and second with regard to *ourselves*. The more we value who God is and who we are, the more our lives will reflect holiness.

WHERE HOLY STARTS Before diving into what holiness looks like in our lives, we must understand God's holiness, because we were created to reflect who he is.

When God says he is holy, he is saying that he is completely and absolutely perfect. His attributes are unique, and he deserves to be worshipped. He is fully God and always God. All of his attributes—his power, his goodness, his love, his truth, his righteousness, his wisdom, his knowledge, and so much more—are infinitely awe-inspiring. He is the only being in the universe who deserves the title God.

There can be an element of *fear* in understanding holiness, in the same sense that you might be awed by the power of a thunderstorm or amazed by the unstoppable force of an avalanche. But there is also *trust* because this immense power is protecting us. There is *excitement* because this awesome presence has a future for us. There is *passion* because this intimate, loving, ever-present source has captivated our hearts. And there is *obedience* because this perfect being inspires our loyalty.

Holy is the term the Bible uses to describe a God who never ceases to amaze us. His actions, words, character, thoughts, motivations, reactions, decisions, and emotions are completely good and completely *God*. He is always true to himself and always committed to us.

It's worth noting that the Hebrew word for holy is *qadosh*, which means "set apart" or "consecrated."[1] The term is religious in origin, which is why *holy* has a religious connotation for us today. Outside of the occasional guacamole reference, of course.

Qadosh describes something that has been chosen or dedicated for a specific purpose. For example, it is used in the Bible to describe utensils in the temple. They were holy, not because they never sinned—they were dishes, after all—but because they were used exclusively in the temple. The term is used for the people who served in the temple, for the same reason: they were the only ones allowed to serve there, and their lives were dedicated to that purpose. The term is also used for Israel in general, as a people set apart for God: a special, valuable, chosen people.[2]

God is *qadosh* as well. How can God be set apart? Because he is always, exclusively, and completely God. He is set apart from creation. He is different from humanity. He is without sin, without evil, without fault. He is separate from anything and everything else in the universe. God is unchanging, unequalled, untouchable. He was and is and always will be God.

It's difficult—maybe even impossible—to embrace holiness for your own life if you don't have a healthy awe for God. When the Bible speaks of his holiness, part of the meaning of that word includes the feelings his presence creates in us. Feelings of absolute, awestruck wonder. Of gratitude and humility and joy and security and submission and triumph and love all rolled into one.

Do you know what that feeling is called? *Worship.*

Sometimes we think of worship as songs or music, but singing is just the audible part of worship. Worship can be expressed with our mouth, but it always starts in our heart. It starts when we see God for who he is and fall in love with him all over again.

So, forget striving to be holier for a moment. Put aside the list of weaknesses you are so embarrassed about. The reasons why you're not good enough. The petitions you want God to answer. The accomplishments that deserve God's attention.

Stop thinking about yourself at all, and instead contemplate God. Just God. Think about his beauty. His love. His mercy. His power. His purity. His creativity. His sense of humor. His forgiveness. His generosity. His passion. Then let your heart and mind, and maybe even your mouth, express your awe. Forget yourself and focus on God.

Your fear and shame, your ego and angst, your striving and restlessness—all dissolve into peace as your gaze stays centered on God. He is holy, and his holiness deserves our worship. It's where holy starts.

IN THE IMAGE OF HOLY Awe, greatness, goodness, purity, uniqueness, sovereignty, majesty—these things and more are contained in the idea of holiness as it applies to God. What about holiness as it applies to us though?

The foundation of all human holiness is this: we are made in God's image. If God is holy, then it follows that humans were created for holiness, and the meaning of holy in our lives should have something to do with the meaning it has in reference to God.

This is important. Holiness is a divine calling, not a human accomplishment. Of course, we can and should participate in fulfilling

HOLINESS IS A DIVINE CALLING, NOT A HUMAN ACCOMPLISHMENT.

that calling and living holy lives, but holy is first and foremost about the God who sets us apart, not about us trying really hard to be good and to do good.

Remember, God is not holy because he follows rules. He makes the rules. He is not holy because he overcomes temptation. According to the Bible, he can't even be tempted in the first place (James 1:13). God is not holy because of what he doesn't do but because of who he is.

The same holds true for us. Our holiness does not spring from our actions but from our *identity*. There's a reason why God calls us his Saints (or "holy ones"). You might be thinking, *I'm no Saint! I'm barely a Christian!* But despite what you may have heard, Saints are not just miracle workers who live in stained glass windows and don't go anywhere without their halos.

Let's look at three things the Bible tells us about Saints.

First, the word *Christian* is used only three times in the New Testament, but the Greek word *hagios* ("Saints") is used over sixty times! And in the Old Testament, the word *Saints* is used to describe the people of God's kingdom (Dan. 7:18, 22, 27 ESV). Sadly, over the years this beautiful identifier has been reduced to a label that bolsters pride and religious elitism.

Second, Paul, the man who wrote nearly half of the New Testament, often began his letters by addressing his audience as Saints.

"To all those in Rome who are loved by God and called to be Saints" (Rom. 1:7 ESV)

"To the church of God that is at Corinth, with all the Saints who are in the whole of Achaia . . ." (2 Cor. 1:1 ESV)

"To the Saints who are in Ephesus . . ." (Eph. 1:1 ESV)

"To the Saints . . . in Colossae . . ." (Col. 1:2 ESV)

We could give more examples, but you get the idea.

When Paul penned these words, he was, for the most part, writing to gentiles and outsiders—people who were considered unworthy or unholy by the religious elite. These letters were originally sent to those who were brand new to this whole following Jesus thing—people who were, in many ways, still making a mess of things. Yet despite all of this, Paul, inspired by God's Spirit, called them Saints. And these words reach through time, inviting us, wherever we find ourselves today, to see ourselves as Saints too.

Third, since God the Father is the Holy One, when he calls us Saints (holy ones), he is speaking identity over his children, reminding us that we are indeed his sons and daughters, re-created in his holiness, and empowered by grace to follow in the footsteps of Jesus, our older brother (Rom. 8:29 and Heb. 2:11).[3]

We are holy because we are his children.

OUR HOLINESS DOES NOT SPRING FROM OUR ACTIONS BUT FROM OUR IDENTITY.

Therefore holiness is not primarily about fear or behavior, but about awe, about uniqueness, about identity, about being set apart by God as his special treasure.

To be holy is to be truly human, and to be human is to reflect the awesomeness and the attributes of a holy God. Holiness does not mean forcing ourselves to live some religious, strict, artificial lifestyle. It's not about *denying* who we really are but *embracing* that identity and allowing our lives to reflect that reality. Holiness is divinity shining through humanity.

God is generous. So when you give freely, you are holy.

God is good. So when you do good works, you are holy.

God is love. So when you love unconditionally, you are holy.

God is pure. So when your actions reflect purity, you are holy.

God is just. So when you stand up against injustice, you are holy.

God is joy. So when you are happy, you are holy.

God is peace. So when you are at rest, you are holy.

God is creative. So when you build, draw, compose, and write, you are holy.

We'll explore some of those thoughts in more detail later on, but for now, realize this—holiness is your calling. It's your gift. And it's your identity as God's creation. You are holy because he is holy and he made you in his image. Don't wait to be perfect before you believe you are holy. That will never happen anyway. Holiness isn't something you have to strain and strive to achieve; it's who you are. God made you holy, and through Jesus he restored you to righteousness. He'll help you live the right way, but he already calls you holy.

Rest in that truth for a minute. Breathe it in.

Sometimes we get so stressed out trying to be something we think we're not, when in reality, it's who we've been all along. We just haven't understood it correctly. To be human is to be holy, and we're never more human than when we walk in holiness.

AWE AND WONDER We've covered how being made in the image of a holy God means we are called to be holy. But practically speaking, what does that look like? What does it mean to be holy? How can we have holy lives? Let's look at three facets of holiness and how they can apply to us practically: holiness as *awesomeness*, holiness as *purpose*, and holiness as *purity*.

First, holiness has to do with awesomeness. God's holiness, as we saw already, is another way of saying he is great, powerful, sovereign, unique, worthy of worship, and so much more. There aren't enough adjectives and superlatives to describe him.

DON'T BE AFRAID, I'VE REDEEMED YOU. I'VE CALLED YOUR NAME. YOU'RE MINE.
(ISA. 43:1 MSG)

As a young person, I didn't understand the truth of this verse. That left me vulnerable, because when you don't know whose you are, you become whatever the world echoes about you. In my case, I traded my priesthood for labels of the world: the wasted, the depressed, the lustful, the player, the bulimic, the people pleaser, and eventually (what made me most ashamed of myself) the cheater. The thing that had broken my parents' marriage and that I had said I would never do, I did.

I was so low and so lost I didn't know where or how to even start again. But when no one else was there for me, Jesus picked up my broken pieces and carried me. He was loyal when I hadn't been. It took time, but change began to come. Chains fell, breakthrough happened, and I learned who I really am in him.

Beyond the labels that this world gives, beyond the suffixes or adjectives that are spoken over or yelled at me, there is one name that is eternal and unchanging: Daughter of God.

I am precious because he bought me with his precious blood. (1 Pet. 1:18–19)

I am worthy because the master of the universe made me perfect in him. (Ps. 139:13–16)

I am loved because he loved me first. (1 John 4:19)

I pray that our heavenly Father will give you the revelation of his love and plans for you. May you see yourself as he sees you, and may you hear all the beautiful and wonderful things that he says about you!

LUCIA BRACHO

The same thing is true of humanity. Think about that for a minute. Humanity, in God's eyes, is awesome. We are the pinnacle of his creation. We were created to reflect his glory and to relate to him as children. It's hard to overstate how important we are to him. God thinks humans are gloriously and infinitely valuable. That is part of what it means to be holy.

The problem, of course, is that we are not always awesome in our behavior. Far from it. If you look at the current condition of society, at wars, at social injustice, at environmental abuse, and at so many other things, it's much easier to see shame than glory.

Those things must change, and the more we as humans reflect God, the more they will change. The problem is not humanity as God created it, but rather the *brokenness* of humanity that has affected us throughout our history. The answer to that brokenness is to return continually to who we were created to be. It's not to be less human but to be more human.

If you've ever been involved in restoring an antique shop treasure or rebuilding and repainting a classic car or remodeling a house that once was majestic but has fallen into ruin, you know what it's like to look beyond appearances and see value. Countless people could have walked past the treasure, car, or house without stopping. They saw abandonment. They saw trash. They saw defects. But you saw value.

Holiness is about value. It's a recognition that something was meant for greatness, regardless of its current state. The message of holiness is that we were created to be important, influential, valuable, and beautiful. We were created to inspire awe and admiration.

EVEN WHEN OUR ACTIONS ARE NOT WHAT GOD INTENDED, OUR VALUE DOES NOT CHANGE.

Things like hatred, violence, fear, and selfishness distort that creation and obscure God's image, but God's creation and design remains. Even when our actions are not what God intended, our value does not change. We were still designed for greatness. And that's still how God sees us.

Human dignity depends on understanding that we are valuable simply because we are human. That is the basis for social justice, after all—the belief that every human is worthy of life, liberty, safety, and freedom of choice; that people matter; that individuals have potential; that everyone should be protected and empowered.

Believe this for yourself. No, you aren't perfect. Yes, you have weaknesses. No, you don't always reflect the beauty you were made for. Yes, you've made mistakes. But you still inspire awe. You are breathtaking. You are beautiful. Heaven applauds you. Your creativity, your work ethic, your love, your laughter, your talents, your accomplishments—they are nothing short of incredible. Your humanity is your glory because you were created in the image of a glorious God.

Why is it so hard to believe that we are valuable? Could it be that we have allowed comparison, competition, and culture to demean us? To shame us, to ridicule us, to disgrace us? To tell us that we start out worthless and we have to prove our value by being better than others or by accomplishing some great thing or by never failing?

We are so quick to point out the flaws in the world and in culture and society, in ourselves and in others. But God says we are special to him. We are valuable to him. We are full of his potential and his gifts and his power.

Let's believe God instead of culture, and let's listen to Jesus instead of shame. Along the way, we'll continue to change those things that blur or distort God's reflection, but not out of self-hatred—rather, out of a recognition of our innate worth.

HOW TO BE HUMAN Not only does holiness imply that something inspires *awe and wonder*, it also implies that it has *purpose*. It's a way of saying that something was designed with a goal in mind.

God is holy because he is fully committed to being God. That is who he is and what he does. Remember the word *qadosh*? We talked about God being "set apart" from creation, from humanity, and from sin. But he's not just set apart *from* certain things, he is also set apart to *be* and *do* certain things.

In his case, it's to be God. And in our case, it's to be human. Holiness means we were designed as humans to function in certain ways and with specific purposes. This is important, because if we want to be holy, we need to know our purpose. Fulfilling that divine calling is the essence of being holy.

Have you ever tried to use something as a screwdriver that wasn't a screwdriver? Maybe you needed to remove the back of a battery cover and you didn't have a screwdriver handy, so you tried your fingernail. That didn't work—it just chipped. So you tried a butter knife. That was too big. So you looked around for something, anything, to remove those aggravating little screws. Eventually you gave up and scoured the house until you found a screwdriver, and in ten seconds the screws were out. Why? Because the screwdriver was designed for one job, one job only—and it does that job really well. But try using the screwdriver to butter or pick up your toast, and you'll be frustrated all over again.

Holiness has to do with living according to your design, with fulfilling your purpose. You are holy when you live out God's intention for you. A big part of life and spirituality is learning what that looks like.

How do you handle your finances?

How do you deal with tragedy?

How do you manage conflict?

How do you choose a career?

How do you respond to authorities?

How do you serve your employees?

How do you love your spouse?

How do you raise your children?

How do you overcome temptation?

How do you live in peace and joy?

Being human is hard. You've probably noticed. It's difficult to know how to respond in certain situations or how to interact with certain people. It's challenging to behave in ways that help people rather than hurt people.

Holiness, therefore, is about being good at being human. It means "human-ing" well. That's the point of the instructions and commands in the Bible. They aren't arbitrary rules. They aren't God being a control freak. They aren't divine strategies to keep life from being exciting. They are invitations, reminders, and directions to making life work. They are cheat codes to hurting people less and loving people more.

God didn't create you to be eye candy but to be an active participant in his plans. You are set apart for God's purposes, and that is close to his heart. What are those purposes? We'll explore that question throughout this book, but they include your career, your family, your relationship with him, your interactions with the world around you, and so much more. His goal for you goes far beyond "not sinning." He wants you to fulfill your potential, to use the gifts he has given you, to experience abundant life, and

YOU ARE HOLY WHEN YOU LIVE OUT GOD'S INTENTION FOR YOU.

to represent him fully in your daily interactions. He wants you to embody his love and truth and to use what you have been given to serve others.

When he calls you holy, he is saying you are created with a purpose. You are set apart for his plans and his use. Only time will tell what that looks like for each one of us, because our callings are as unique as our fingerprints and our faces. But two things are certain: God knew what he was doing when he made you, and he knows what he is doing as he leads you down the pathway of life.

PURELY HUMAN Finally, let's look at holiness as *purity*. At first glance, purity sounds like the stereotypical, rules-based view of holiness: obeying the Bible, avoiding sin, overcoming temptation. But it's not.

The Bible's definition of holy focuses on being completely committed or consecrated to one thing. God is a *holy* God because he is *wholly* God. He is always God and nothing but God. There is nothing about him that is not fully God. He has no mixture, no compromise, no impurity. Holiness for humans, therefore, should reflect that same kind of consistency or purity.

In church and in Christian contexts, the word *purity* (like the word *holiness*) often gets reduced to rules about sexuality or other behavior. But that's not the meaning of purity—it's just one of the areas where purity is important.

Purity is wholeness. Completeness. Integrity of substance. Purity is about being fully human.

To put it another way, purity is a positive thing. It's defined by what you are, not by what you are not; by what you do, not by what you don't do. Pure water tastes good because it's completely, fully water. Anything that were to contaminate it would affect the taste. Pure gold is valuable because it's completely, fully gold. Anything that were to be mixed in would reduce its value. The water and the gold are the focus because they are innately good or valuable. In the same way, purity is about being who you are, nothing more and nothing less. The value lies in being you, and that is exactly what holiness refers to.

Sin is impurity because it was not part of our original design. God did not create us to sin. He didn't set us apart to sin. He didn't call us to sin. Rather, he created us, set us apart, and called us to holiness. And as we saw above, holiness means maximizing our humanity and living our lives according to God's purposes.

Sin is an interloper and a distraction. Jesus told his disciples that the Enemy comes to "steal and kill and destroy" (John 10:10), and that is what sin does. Regardless of the momentary pleasure or profit it might bring, ultimately it takes from us, and that is why it is sin.

It's really not complicated. The problem is, we think we can game the system. We think we can have just a little bit of sin, a little bit of impurity, a little bit of mixture, without losing anything in the process. But by definition, sin isn't worth it. How could it be? It runs contrary to who we were created to be.

Ironically, calling something sin sometimes increases its attractiveness. If you are told not to do something, you often want to do it even more, precisely because you were told not to. Sometimes that is simply *pride*: the desire we have in ourselves to be our own boss. Sometimes it's *lust*: the desire to feel or achieve something prohibited. Sometimes it's *fear*: the emotion that we might lose something if we don't act now. Sometimes it's *addiction*: the irresistible drive to do what we know is harmful. Sometimes it's *greed*: the desire to have more and more of something. Regardless, it's harmful, and sooner or later it will cause regret.

The fight against sin is not easy. The Bible doesn't hide from that reality, but it doesn't make excuses for it either. Rather, it provides the solution: Jesus.

If you want to know what humanity was meant to look like, look at Jesus. He was fully human and fully God. His years on earth were a living, breathing example of what it means to experience life and live free from sin.

That doesn't mean Jesus was some angelic android, devoid of emotion or spontaneity. If you read the biblical narrative, you find someone who loved life, who cultivated deep friendships, who left an indelible impact on those around him, who fought for justice and for good, who won the love and trust of many, who stood up boldly to corruption, who believed in people, who forgave and healed and loved, and who had a sharp sense of humor. Jesus was pure and holy, and because of that he lived life to the fullest.

I'D BEEN DATING THE LOVE OF MY LIFE FOR FOUR YEARS. WE DID MINISTRY TOGETHER, SPENT TIME WITH EACH OTHER'S FAMILIES, AND PLANNED A FUTURE TOGETHER. I THOUGHT OUR RELATIONSHIP WAS INVINCIBLE, SECURE, AND SURE, UNTIL THE DAY I GOT THAT PHONE CALL.

"I'm just not in love with you anymore," he said. My heart sank. "You're just not what I'm looking for." I sat there, confused. "I'm just not happy." Tears began to roll down my face.

I refused to accept it at first. I spent months trying to fix the relationship, begging him not to leave me, desperately looking for a "cure" so he would love me again. I was angry and confused. We both loved God. We had tried to do everything right, to be godly and pure. I never anticipated the relationship would fail. Other friends had similar relationships that resulted in engagements and beautiful weddings. I wanted the same. I wanted to be able to show off my diamond ring and to have that Instagrammable marriage. I thought if I fought hard enough for it, I could get the image I longed for. It didn't work.

When I finally had to accept the truth, my heart was shattered. I wept for days, crying out to God. And there, in a moment of stillness with him, I learned a lesson that would reshape my life: what I thought I needed and what God has for me are two totally different things. His purposes don't always align with our own plans or wants, but they are always better. I invested so much of my heart, time, and energy into something that was never from God. I let my expectations guide me instead of his voice. I let my pride and human desires control my decisions instead of letting him be in control.

I found healing, not by finding a new relationship, not by becoming angry at the person who broke my heart, and not by creating new expectations. I found healing by setting my heart free from the shackles of my own desires. Today I live a life guided by my Creator. I serve him, not because of what he can do for me but because it's why I was created. Of course, I still hope to one day get married, have a family, and accomplish my dreams, but ultimately all of that is secondary in the big scheme of why I was created. I was created to serve, worship, and honor my King.

I urge you to do the same. Pursue him fervently and passionately. In moments of disappointment, simply seek him, draw close to who he is, be still in his presence, and lay it down. Lay down your own expectations and simply be ready for God to move in your life like never before.

GABRIELLA ASPURU

He didn't just live, of course. He died. For us. Through his death, his holiness and righteousness passed to us, as we'll see in the next chapter.

Now, sin cannot change our status. Because of Jesus, we are righteous, accepted, and holy. And sin cannot control our lives, because Jesus offers us grace to stand against temptation and to embrace the life God created for us. In other words, Jesus is both our source of forgiveness and our source of strength to resist sin. We are holy because he made us holy, and we are holy because he helps us live in holiness.

Living in holiness and purity is not always easy, but the result is always worth it. Holiness is far better than the alternative: allowing sin to reign in us, to steal from us, to water down our humanity, to tarnish the reflection of God, to turn our love to fear, to replace our boldness with shame.

Look to Jesus. Let him lead the way. Receive his grace, depend on him, trust him, listen to him, and obey him. The closer you come to Jesus, the more you will experience his gift of abundant, pure humanity.

How about you? Do you see God as holy? Do you see yourself as holy? Are you living in holiness?

Maybe you only see your failures, your weaknesses, your mistakes.

Maybe you feel holy only when you're on a good streak . . . which is rare.

Maybe you think holiness is for an elite few.

Maybe you think holiness is something you earn.

Maybe you think holiness is something God holds against you because you've never quite arrived.

None of those things are true. You are holy right now, through Jesus, no matter what your past might say. You belong to Jesus. You were created in God's image for great things. You are accepted, set apart, chosen, called, gifted, valued, and celebrated.

I am holy. It's a statement of identity and of value. It's an affirmation of the victory of Jesus in you and through you. It's a declaration of your choice to identify with God and to reflect him. It's an affirmation of your value in God's eyes and your role in God's plan.

God calls you holy, and nothing can change that.

I AM HOLY, so I stand out from the crowd. I recognize that holiness is so much more than "following the rules." Holiness is not an attempt to just be good enough. Rather, it's my journey of embracing everything my Father has for me. A journey into the beauty, wonder, and majesty of what it is to be a child of God and share in his nature. It's his nature within that makes me stand out. God's holiness transforms every area of my life. And because of his Spirit and grace, I can be holy—in thought, word, and deed. To be holy is to be whole. To be holy is to be his. I am holy, *so I stand out from the crowd.*

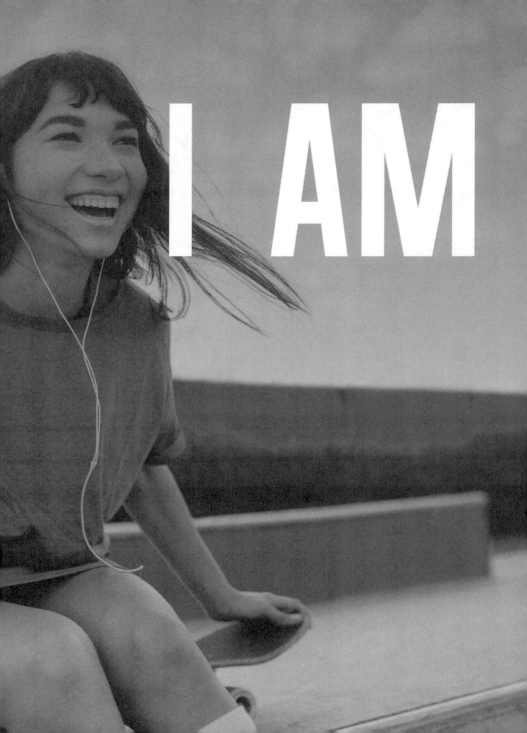

RIGHTEOUS

HAVE YOU EVER SEEN A COMPANY offer a free gift as part of some marketing campaign? Buy a makeup kit and you'll get a special brush for free or purchase a laptop and get free headphones or sign up for an email list and get a free e-book. The phrase *free gift* has a few problems though.

First, it's redundant. Gifts are always free—literally by definition. If it's not free, it's not a gift. So when a company insists that this isn't just your average, run-of-the-mill gift but a *free* gift, the very fact they felt compelled to emphasize the word *free* should raise suspicion.

Second, it's usually not true. Whatever they are offering is not free. It's some sort of marketing ploy. Even if all they ask for is your email address, they still want something: your inbox, your attention, your name on a list they're going to turn around and sell to someone else who will invade your privacy with spam until

Jesus comes back. They are hoping to sell you more products or services, and the gift is bait to get you hooked.

Third, free gifts are usually accompanied by fine print. You've seen it—the little asterisk at the end of the offer, indicating that "some terms and conditions may apply." If you do take the time to look up the terms and conditions, you usually find that the word *some* should be *many*. A list filled with technicalities and legalese specifies who qualifies and who doesn't. And often, there is a time limit. You get a thirty-day free trial, then they trap you with sneaky credit card payments you can't figure out how to cancel.

Now, in all fairness, there are nonprofit organizations and good-hearted people out there who literally want to help people by giving them some item, service, or information for free, which is great. But typically they give away whatever it is *without* plastering free gift all over their advertising in a cringey boldface font that's in all caps with four exclamation marks.

Retailers and marketers aren't the only ones who give gifts that aren't really free. Maybe you have a family member or friend who tends to hold gifts they've given you, or favors they've done for you, over your head. Maybe they expect a favor in return or your time or your affection. It doesn't feel good at all. Those things are not really gifts, because you end up paying for them in some way. There's a hook. There's a catch. There's a condition.

Gifts that have strings attached are so common in our culture that it's easy, even smart, to be suspicious when we are offered something for free. Whether it's family, friends, companies, employers, or even God, we often conclude that "nothing is free."

The Bible also talks about a "free gift." It's the gift of righteousness and eternal life that we receive through faith in Jesus. Romans 6:23 says this: "For the wages of sin is death, but the *free gift* of God is eternal life in Christ Jesus our Lord" (ESV, italics added). Earlier in the same book, Paul wrote about God giving us "the *free gift* of righteousness" (5:17 ESV, italics added).

In defense of the apostle Paul, the original Greek text is not redundant in labeling the gift as free. The original text uses *charisma*, a Greek word for gift that is often connected to God's graciousness and goodness.[1] Certain Bible translations add the word *free*, probably to emphasize how good, how divine, how generous this gift actually is. Why? Precisely because we are cynical. We have a tough time believing that righteousness and eternal life could be given to us so freely.

And yet, God's gift of righteousness is truly a gift, with no strings or conditions attached. It's not empty hype, he's not trying to sell you something, no one is excluded, and there is no

GOD'S GIFT OF RIGHTEOUSNESS IS TRULY A GIFT, WITH NO STRINGS OR CONDITIONS ATTACHED.

time limit on his offer. Out of the goodness of his heart and in compassion for humanity, God offers forgiveness, righteousness, and salvation.

Human nature being what it is, though, we tend to forget that gifts are free and righteousness cannot be earned, and we assume this applies to Jesus's gift as well. Now, this doesn't always happen right away. When we first approach God, we probably accept the gift of salvation with gratitude and faith. But as time goes on, we start to think that while our initial salvation was free, the rest of life is going to cost something: our obedience, our sacrifice, our holiness, our religiosity, our fervor, our service.

To put it another way, we reduce God's gift to a trial offer. "Try righteousness free for thirty days, then live the rest of your life under the thumb of fear." But that's not freedom. That's not a gift. If we think righteousness is something we have to deserve and preserve, to earn and protect, we've forgotten what free really means.

As has often been pointed out, righteousness is a gift to us, but that doesn't mean it was free to God. It cost Jesus his life. Salvation is an infinitely valuable gift because Jesus paid for it on the cross. But then he gave that salvation to us, freely and generously and completely. He isn't going to send us a bill later, and he isn't going to hold it over our head. Jesus died to save us, and it is his desire and his expectation that we receive his gift, not with fear or promises to repay but with gratitude, faith, and worship.

HOW GOD LOVED So if God's gift to us is righteousness, what exactly does that mean? The word itself is often understood strictly as a legal term that refers to right standing, justice, and uprightness. It has to do with doing what is right and not doing what is wrong, which results in good standing before the law and society. In modern language, it largely means having a clean record with the law versus having a criminal record.

Since God is the source of right and wrong, he is the ultimate standard. He determines who is righteous, or who has right standing before him and who doesn't. Unfortunately, none of us qualifies on our own because we've all sinned and fallen short of the glory that he designed us to know and enjoy (Rom. 3:23). We all have a record, so when we stand before an all-knowing judge, we can't claim innocence, for all of us have missed the mark.

While this forensic or legal idea of righteousness isn't necessarily wrong, there is a deeper meaning and more personal dimension to the word that shouldn't be ignored.

Ultimately, righteousness always has been and always will be the badge of the people of God. It is our family emblem—the sign that we are his. It is the language that God used with Abraham when he cryptically promised to bless all the families of the world by them becoming part of Abraham's family. And because of the eternal faithfulness of Jesus Christ, the Son who was faithful even when humanity proved unfaithful, we are now righteous *in him*, as members of God's true and eternal family.

So, yes, the word *righteousness* contains a transactional or legal component, but more importantly, it invites us into a story of *belonging*, a belonging that does not ebb and flow with our successes and failures. A belonging that is grounded in the covenant faithfulness of Jesus Christ, the One who is righteousness incarnate, the perfect intersection of God's faithfulness to us and humanity's faithfulness to God, the bridge that reconciles the children to the Father's heart.

God deeply loves us and desires intimacy with us. The biblical narrative begins and ends with a wedding for a reason. We were created for the depths of love, and just because we chose a different path doesn't mean God gave up on us. That's where the gospel—a word that means "good news"—comes in. The gospel is about God's plan to reconcile the world to himself.

The message of the gospel is simple. All of us have sinned, meaning we violated relationship with God, ourselves, and each other. Because the penalty for sin is death—not just physical death but eternal, spiritual death—we needed someone to save us from the isolation and disorientation that come with sin. God loves

THE GOSPEL IS ABOUT GOD'S PLAN TO RECONCILE THE WORLD TO HIMSELF.

all of humanity, and he made a way for us to become "dead to sin" and for our relationship with him to be restored through his Son (Rom. 8:11 ESV). Jesus is God, but he became a human and lived among humanity. He never sinned; instead, he took our sins upon himself and died in our place. Then he rose again, proving that death itself (the penalty for sin) had been conquered. Jesus overcame sin and death and the devil and guilt and shame and addiction and every other negative, sin-related thing, and *he did that for us*.

There are a lot of theological nuances and truths wrapped up in those sentences, but they can be summed up by maybe the most famous verse of the Bible, John 3:16. "For this is how God loved the world: He gave his one and only Son, so that everyone who believes in him will not perish but have eternal life" (NLT). God is the giver, and we are the recipients.

This gift of salvation was not given on a whim. God didn't just randomly decide to rescue humanity one day. Ever since the garden of Eden, when Adam and Eve brought sin into the world, God was working and planning toward Jesus's victory. Why? Because while he can't overlook sin, which is the antithesis of who he is, he didn't want to give up on us either. God is love, and love doesn't give up. It can't give up.

This salvation motivated by love is one of the main themes of the Bible. One of the most important demonstrations of this is, as we mentioned earlier, the story of Abraham, whom the New Testament called "the father of all who believe" (Rom. 4:11). He is a key figure in the biblical story of God's gift of righteousness.

God asked Abraham to trust him, to follow him, and to believe his promises. The Bible says Abraham "believed the Lord, and the Lord counted him as righteous because of his faith" (Gen. 15:6 NLT). In other words, his righteousness was a result of his faith.

From Abraham, his son Isaac, and then Isaac's son Jacob, God raised up the nation of Israel. Israel was God's people of promise and another key piece in God's plan to restore righteousness and save humanity. God made a covenant with Israel, a pact based on promises. He called them to be his people, and he committed to be their God. He was with them, he blessed them, and he gave them spiritual truths and understanding. He created a religious system of laws and sacrifices designed to deal with their sin, at least temporarily, and to point them toward a future Messiah, who would solve the sin issue once and for all.

When Jesus was born, it was the culmination of a grand plan that spanned millennia. He is the Messiah. He is the answer to humanity's sin and separation from God. He is the source of salvation for all. The law, the psalms, and the prophets were pointing to him. The righteousness Abraham received and the forgiveness Israel found in their sacrifices pointed to the righteousness and forgiveness we now receive in Jesus. From Abraham to Israel to Jesus, God was working to solve the problem of sin and to restore our relationship with him—a relationship unfettered by guilt or shame or condemnation.

As we look at the effort and planning God put into giving us this gift of righteousness, it's important to realize three things.

God Wanted to Save Us   That is why he took the initiative to seek and save us. It was his plan, his work, his Son, his sacrifice, and his forgiveness.

Remember Jesus's statement in John 3:16? "This is how God loved." He loved us so he saved us, and his salvation proves his love. The fact that God actively desired and pursued our salvation is a clear statement about our value to him, especially when we aren't convinced we are worth that much ourselves or when we're going through difficult moments and God seems absent. We can start to think he's disappointed in us or he's forgotten about us or he doesn't care about us or he quit loving us. But if he cared enough to send Jesus, don't you think you can trust his love even in the hard seasons, even when you can't see or feel it? Jesus gave his life—that's the greatest gift anyone can give. Difficult circumstances don't mean his love has failed. On the contrary, hard times will often reveal his love more clearly than ever. Lean into his love and trust his heart toward you.

God Alone Can Save Us   Not only did God want to save us but he was the only one who could save us. We couldn't save ourselves, and we had nothing to offer God in exchange. That's why righteousness is a gift, not a trade or a bargain or an agreement or a loan. Again, that statement is true throughout our lives, not just at the moment of salvation. We can't allow the thought to creep in that we somehow have to start "earning our keep" now that we are saved. We didn't earn our righteousness by our works, and we can't maintain our righteousness by our works either.

God Did Save Us His salvation is effective. His sacrifice was successful. He did for us what we could not do for ourselves. Paul wrote, "But God showed his great love for us by sending Christ to die for us while we were still sinners" (Rom. 5:8 NLT). We don't have to wait and see if we are holy enough: we have been made righteous by God through faith, and we stand firm in that knowledge.

God wants you to know and believe that he has made you righteous. It's his deep desire that you be in relationship with him, free from fear and guilt. Righteousness is his declaration and his work. No matter what might be going on around you, no matter what you might be facing or struggling with, and no matter what weaknesses or fears have gotten you down, God still calls you righteous.

Hold your head high. Breathe deeply. Open your heart. You are righteous.

THE END OF SHAME One of the reasons it is so important to know you are righteous is because it is the best way to counteract the power of shame.

Have you ever had a sudden flashback to a humiliating moment from your past? Maybe you're just drifting off to sleep when you

HOLD YOUR HEAD HIGH.
BREATHE DEEPLY. OPEN YOUR HEART.
YOU ARE RIGHTEOUS.

randomly recall that day in fourth grade when you made a fool of yourself in front of the entire class. Or maybe you're eating breakfast, thinking about nothing in particular, when something triggers the memory of that time you tried to ask someone out and ended up putting your foot so far into your mouth you still haven't gotten it out. Those flashbacks have the power to awaken all the terror and shame of the original event—plus some.

Shame, according to the Oxford dictionary, is "a painful feeling of humiliation or distress caused by the consciousness of wrong or foolish behavior."[2] Shame is a powerful emotion that drives a wedge between us and God and often between us and other people as well.

The reason shame is so hard to shake is because it flows from our knowledge of our own mistakes. We did something wrong, and we feel terrible about it. We can't hide from it, we can't deny it, and we can't fix it. Maybe we convince other people that we haven't done anything wrong, but inside, we are slowly being eaten up by shame.

That's not a healthy way to live, in case you were wondering. You don't have to be a psychologist to see how damaging the weight of secret guilt can be. It's certainly not allowing you to live an abundant life, which is how Jesus described the lifestyle he wants to help us have (John 10:10).

The funny thing about shame—and it's not funny at all—is that it is mostly self-imposed. Yes, there can be cultures of shame, we can be the targets of shaming, and there are people who seem to delight in heaping shame upon others. But ultimately, the choice to be shamed is up to each of us. We are the only ones who can allow the mistakes we've made, or the words others have said to us, to lodge themselves in our thoughts and define our self-identity.

How can we live free from shame? Not by denying our sin—that is impossible. Even our subconscious agrees that we have made some colossal mistakes. Hence the flashbacks.

Freedom from shame can only come by disconnecting our identity from our actions. Who we are and what we are worth should not be determined by what we do or don't do.

WHO WE ARE AND WHAT WE ARE WORTH SHOULD NOT BE DETERMINED BY WHAT WE DO OR DON'T DO.

So what do we base our identity and worth on? On Jesus. On the righteousness he gives us through faith. The fact that we have been granted righteousness means we don't have to be ashamed before God. Yes, that's hard to process because we all know that isn't fair. We've sinned. We've hurt people. We've followed our own lusts and desires. We've said things, done things, looked at things, and taken things that deeply embarrass us now, far more than the embarrassment of our flubbed attempt at asking someone out.

None of those things change the reality of our righteousness, though, because none of those things are the basis for our righteousness in the first place. Jesus is. His work on the cross determined, once and for all, that our slate is clean. We are forgiven, justified, and declared innocent. We are righteous, and shame no longer needs to have power over us.

Yes, there is a place for repentance, for change, for restitution. The righteousness God gives us doesn't erase the natural consequences of our mistakes. But we don't have to wallow in guilt and shame before God. We don't have to live in terror, afraid that God is going to flick us off the planet any second because we shoplifted fifteen years ago or lied to our boss fifteen minutes ago.

That doesn't mean, of course, that we sin willfully or wantonly, as if sin doesn't matter. In the last chapter, we discussed the concept of purity. We looked at purity as an expression of wholeness and congruence. Being pure means being fully human, and sin undermines our humanness.

SHAME IS NOT YOUR FRIEND, AND NEITHER IS HIDING YOUR FAULTS.

But the point of God's gift of righteousness is that even when we *don't* live in purity, we are still righteous before God. Our standing before him comes from Jesus and Jesus alone, not whether we measure up to some standard of behavior.

Now, God won't ignore or enable our sin. Rather, he will confront and correct it, because he loves us and wants us to stop hurting ourselves and others. But since our guilt has already been dealt with on the cross, our standing before him is not ever in question. He loves us, he accepts us, he forgives us, and he believes in us.

Shame is not your friend, and neither is hiding your faults. Neither one is necessary. Instead, run to righteousness. God's righteousness, which he gives to you. Trust his love and acceptance. Believe he has made you blameless. Then face your flaws and weaknesses humbly, make changes as needed, and grow into your abundant life.

CONFIDENT CLOSENESS Once shame is dealt with, we are free to approach God boldly. Why? Because we have nothing to fear and nothing to be ashamed of, we have the confidence to draw close to God. The author of Hebrews wrote, "Let us then approach God's throne of grace with confidence, so that we may receive mercy and find grace to help us in our time of need" (4:16).

This attitude of confident closeness is the essence of prayer. It's the belief that we are welcome in God's presence. That he wants us to be with him, to speak with him, to depend on him. Where shame causes us to hide from God, righteousness causes us to seek God.

So often prayer is reduced, both in our minds and in common religious practice, to something formulaic, external, and somber. We treat prayer as a duty. It's something that pleases God, so we must do it, even though we can hardly stay awake, and secretly we wonder why we're telling an omniscient God things he already knows.

But that isn't prayer at all. Prayer is more about heart than words, it's more about motive than eloquence, and it's more about love than duty. Prayer should not be fearful but rather

WHERE SHAME CAUSES US TO HIDE FROM GOD, RIGHTEOUSNESS CAUSES US TO SEEK GOD.

confident, because we are speaking with the God who chose us, saved us, and loves us unconditionally. Prayer should not be a ritual but rather a spontaneous expression of our heart. Prayer should not be boring or repetitive but rather alive, authentic, and fresh.

There may be moments when you spend an extended amount of time in prayer, but those are the exception. Most prayers are short, sweet, and to the point. The most famous prayer in the Bible, called the Lord's Prayer because it was prayed by Jesus himself, is a mere ten lines long (Matt. 6:9–13). Prayer is less about form and more about motivation and content. You aren't fooling God anyway—he knows exactly what's in your heart and on your mind, and that's what he cares about.

You can pray at a traffic light.

You can pray in line at the grocery store.

You can pray for a parking space in the rain.

You can pray for someone who randomly popped into your mind.

You can pray before a job interview.

You can pray *during* a job interview, but probably don't do it out loud.

You can pray for someone who just expressed a need or fear—often it's better than advice anyway.

You can pray when you're trying to fall asleep at night and your mind won't slow down.

You can pray when the world seems out of control, or rather when *your* world seems out of control.

You can pray for a spouse, and you can pray to be a better spouse.

You can pray with gratitude when you're happy.

You can pray with anger when life has betrayed you.

You can pray with grief when tragedy strikes.

You can pray when you don't even know what to pray or how to pray, just by surrendering to God's will.

There are a million reasons and times to pray. Just don't pray to impress God or to manipulate him or because you're scared that he's mad at you or because you think you deserve something. Those are self-focused approaches that ultimately undermine the very nature of prayer. Confident closeness is less about getting what you want from God and more about simply wanting God. It's

CONFIDENT CLOSENESS IS LESS ABOUT GETTING WHAT YOU WANT FROM GOD AND MORE ABOUT SIMPLY WANTING GOD.

about trusting in him and surrendering to him, knowing that he responds to your needs and desires because he loves you.

IN JESUS'S NAME One of the reasons we might view prayer as a formula is because we often follow a formula when we pray. We don't mean to, maybe, it's just how it's always done. You start with a "Dear Jesus" or "Dear Heavenly Father," as if you are writing a thank-you note to your grandparents for a Christmas gift they gave you. Next you list out your requests and maybe a few complaints or expressions of gratitude. Then you close the prayer with this phrase or something similar: "In Jesus's name, amen." And for those times when you are feeling extra spiritual or especially desperate, you might have learned to throw in a few adjectives: "In Jesus's precious, powerful, holy name, amen."

There's nothing wrong with all that, but we miss the point of prayer if we think it has to be that way, if we believe that filler words and catchphrases are the essence of prayer. They are not. Closeness is, as we saw above. Prayer is about drawing close to God in confidence, as sons and daughters who are loved and righteous in his eyes. You can start your prayer how you want, you can include what you want, and you can end it however you want. You can pray as short or as long, as soft or as loud, as simply or as eloquently as you need to. Just read the book of Psalms. You'll find the entire gamut of human emotion and experience illustrated in poetic prayers.

THE PRAYER OF A PERSON LIVING RIGHT WITH GOD IS SOMETHING POWERFUL TO BE RECKONED WITH.
(JAMES 5:16 MSG)

I was blessed to have parents who intentionally taught me that, as a daughter of God, I can boldly come before Him in prayer. They not only taught me that, but they showed it too. We prayed together daily as a family, and it was our first response to any kind of need or crisis. My parents were so faithful in prayer, and we saw many of those prayers answered. Both my brother and I had severe asthma as kids. We had to get up several times a night to use our inhalers because we were wheezing so badly. Day after day, we prayed for healing. At first nothing changed, so we kept on praying. Still nothing changed. But one day, we received prayer again for it, and that time we were healed. We haven't wheezed or needed inhalers since. This fueled my faith. I knew without a shadow of a doubt that God answers prayer.

On another occasion, my dad had severe internal bleeding. The operating surgeon didn't expect him to live. I was eight, and I remember crying and praying myself to sleep. Our church family stayed up all night praying for him. He survived the operation, but the doctors still expected him to die. We kept praying, and he made it through and began to recover. We were told he could expect only a low quality of life after the operation, but he recovered so well that he took up running. He regularly ran 5–10k races for the next fifteen years, until he became ill and passed away in August 2018, eighteen years after being told he would certainly die.

HANNAH O'NEILL

There is one little phrase we often repeat that is especially important, although we tend to use it wrong: "in Jesus's name." Jesus himself taught his disciples that they should pray in his name (John 14:13–14), but he never taught them that it was to be the exclusive and essential parting phrase for every prayer. Humans made that up. Jesus prayed a lot, but we never hear him ending with "in my name, amen." For that matter, not a single prayer in the Bible includes this phrase at the end. The closest is Acts 3:6, where Peter commands a lame man, "In the name of Jesus Christ of Nazareth, walk!" But the rest of the prayers we find sound a lot like people talking to God rather than invoking some mystical formula. Again, it's not wrong to pray that way, but let's not miss the point of the phrase. "In Jesus's name" is not a formula we tack on the end like some legal disclaimer.

What is the point? It comes back to righteousness. It comes back to who gives us the right to approach God in prayer in the first place. We don't pray on the basis of our merit but on Jesus's merit. To say we pray in Jesus's name is an affirmation that we are drawing near and praying boldly because Jesus made us righteous, and we have nothing to fear. It's not a phrase we say as much as it is a reality we live in. Jesus was encouraging his disciples to approach God with the same confidence, boldness, security, and trust that he demonstrated in his own prayer life.

In the same way, we relate to God with childlike confidence, as a son or daughter with a loving father. We don't have to live in fear of God or hide in shame from our mistakes, because when God sees us, he sees Jesus. Our sins have been covered, our guilt removed, our shame cast into the sea. The prophet Micah wrote, "You will again have compassion on us; you will tread our sins underfoot and hurl all our iniquities into the depths of the sea" (7:19).

Who we are, how we live, what we hope for, why we are able to have faith for the future—all that and much more come through Jesus.

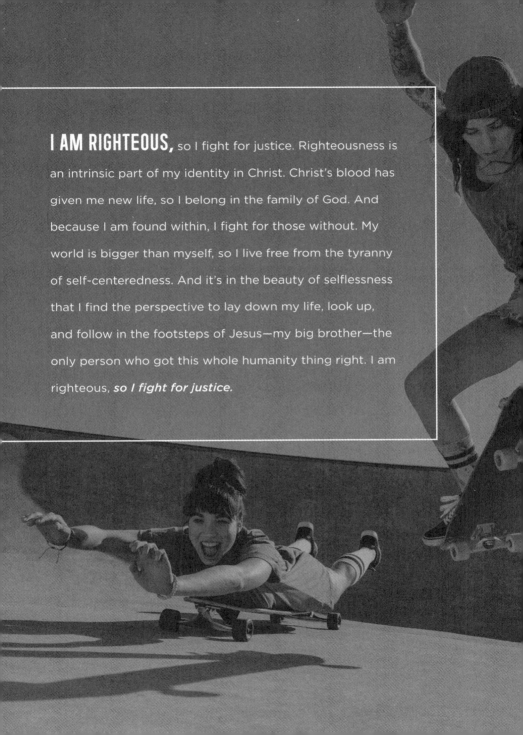

I AM RIGHTEOUS, so I fight for justice. Righteousness is an intrinsic part of my identity in Christ. Christ's blood has given me new life, so I belong in the family of God. And because I am found within, I fight for those without. My world is bigger than myself, so I live free from the tyranny of self-centeredness. And it's in the beauty of selflessness that I find the perspective to lay down my life, look up, and follow in the footsteps of Jesus—my big brother—the only person who got this whole humanity thing right. I am righteous, *so I fight for justice.*

LOVED

IF AN EXTRATERRESTRIAL SCIENTIST ever surveyed Planet Earth, they might come to the conclusion that we have an inexplicable fascination with boxes. They would note that juvenile humans construct rudimentary fortifications from boxes, felines climb into boxes to hide from those same juvenile humans, and adult humans place all kinds of items into boxes and then send them back and forth to each other or just shove them into their garages. They would discover there are entire organizations whose purpose seems to be putting items into boxes and sending them to other humans. They would marvel that many humans even have a ritual where they kill a tree, set it up in their home, then place brightly wrapped boxes all around its decorated remains, like some sort of offering. Earthlings, they would assume, really, really like boxes.

What that alien researcher wouldn't know, however, is that our fascination with boxes extends far beyond the corrugated paper products we use to store and ship items. We often put people in boxes. And ourselves. And even God. We have this unexplainable urge to understand, classify, quantify, explain, and define everything and everybody.

This desire to define is positive in many contexts: it helps us make sense of natural phenomena around us, it gives us a shared set of concepts with which to communicate, and it gives science teachers unending material on which to draw as they design pop quizzes that will haunt our nightmares for decades after the material itself has been forgotten.

But when it comes to relationships, our desire to put others into convenient little boxes is destined for failure. Nowhere is this truer than when we try to understand God himself. Theologians have spent centuries systematically organizing what we know about God in order to construct a coherent and complete picture of him. Unfortunately, their chances of success are about as great as that of those little humans constructing a cardboard fortress that will withstand their mother's command to "clean up this mess!" Some forces just can't be repelled, and some things just can't be fully defined.

When God inspired the Bible, he didn't do it in the form of a textbook. Instead, it's more like a series of journals and stories from people learning to walk with God in their own lives. One of those people, a disciple of Jesus's named John, summed up the complexity and grandeur of God's nature, character, and power in one succinct phrase: "God is love" (1 John 4:8).

Notice he didn't just say, "God is loving" (although that is true), or "God loves you and me" (also true). He said God *is* love. Love isn't just an action or an emotion coming from God, it is part of his very essence. Every aspect of God's nature and every action he takes is consistent with true, eternal love.

We'll unpack what that means for us in the rest of this chapter. If you are bold enough to embrace it, it is nothing short of revolutionary.

LOVED AND LOVING Every one of us needs to feel loved. That's not a weakness of the human race or a shameful chink in our self-protective armor. It's not something we grow out of once we reach adulthood. It's part of who we are—children of God made in his image. We were created to be loved. Our insecurities and sinful responses might distort that need at times, and the sinfulness or foolishness of others might take advantage of it. But the basic

EVERY ASPECT OF GOD'S NATURE AND EVERY ACTION HE TAKES IS CONSISTENT WITH TRUE, ETERNAL LOVE.

WE WERE CREATED TO BE LOVED.

need to be loved is good and godly, a gift from the Father of life and the author of love. The desire to be loved brings energy and strength and joy to our relationships.

As well as being loved, each of us needs to love others. Not in the grudging, "I really don't like them, but I love them since the Bible says I have to" sense, but in the truest sense of the idea. We were designed to love others—to want the best for them, to serve them, to be committed to them, and to be close to them. This aspect of love is also part of who we are as image bearers of our Father. In the same passage where John said, "God is love," he also reminded us, "Let us love one another, for love comes from God" (1 John 4:7). The ability to love others and the very concept of love itself come from God.

We are created to be loved. We are created to love. And both loving and being loved bring life and wonder and joy into our lives.

WHAT IS LOVE? Probably no topic under the sun has been the subject of more songs, poems, movies, or literature than love. Humans are fascinated by it (even more than our fascination with boxes, possibly). Ironically, that fixation on love still hasn't helped us be very good at it. In fact, many of those songs and poems and movies are about *failing* at love. And most of us have more than enough personal stories about our own failings at love to vouch for its complexity.

Part of our problem is that love itself is often misunderstood in our culture. It gets reduced to an emotion, confused with lust, or twisted into something it was never intended to be. We often fail to love others well, or to receive love ourselves, because we misunderstand love itself.

God is the author of love and the epitome of love, so it makes sense to base our understanding of love on his. That's where the Bible comes in. The entire Bible has been compared to a love letter from God to us. (Although we would not suggest taking this too literally when trying to impress someone you are interested in romantically. Sending messages that include genealogies and dietary restrictions isn't going to end well for you.)

WE OFTEN FAIL TO LOVE OTHERS WELL, OR TO RECEIVE LOVE OURSELVES, BECAUSE WE MISUNDERSTAND LOVE ITSELF.

Love as God intended it is emotional, but it's not *only* an emotion. In popular culture love is often reduced to a powerful feeling that fuels a relationship. When the feeling ends, so does the relationship. Christians sometimes swing to the opposite extreme: we emphasize the self-sacrificial nature of love so strongly that our implicit suggestion seems to be that emotions don't matter.

The truth is more complex—and far more beautiful—than the caricatures of love expressed by those two extremes. In the Bible, love is brimming with emotion and passion. Romantic love is expressed in such explicit terms in Song of Solomon that many red-faced church leaders over the centuries have tried to explain away the entire book as merely a metaphor of Christ's love for his church. The lyrics where the two lovers take turns describing each other's body parts usually get skipped completely during Sunday morning sermons.

And it's not just romantic love that is emotional. God's love for his children—even when they are actively rebelling against him—is expressed in such passionate terms in the Bible that you can feel his yearning to be with them and his agony at the way they have rejected him. Love, then, includes emotion.

Along with that emotion, love is a choice. It is a decision to act in ways that serve the person being loved. It is a commitment to value and serve and care for and lift up the other person. A relationship will not succeed if love is defined only by its emotional component. But when we see love as both emotion and choice, passion and commitment, desire and devotion, then it is indeed a foundation for relationships that last.

In 1 Corinthians 13:4–8, the apostle Paul gave us a picture of love that is shocking both in its boldness and its scope:

> Love is patient, love is kind. It does not envy, it does not boast, it is not proud. It does not dishonor others, it is not self-seeking, it is not easily angered, it keeps no record of wrongs. Love does not delight in evil but rejoices with the truth. It always protects, always trusts, always hopes, always perseveres.
>
> Love never fails.

This passage describes a love that is unbreakable, that perseveres through the messiness of relationships, that is fully committed to the one who is loved, and that gives sacrificially and unreservedly. Let's look at what this means for us, the ones God loves.

LOVE IS STRONG God's love is unbreakable. It is stronger than any opposing force. Look back at the passage above. God's love *always* perseveres. It *never* fails. Stop for a second and think about that. It's incredible! Now, say this sentence to yourself: "I am loved." Say it again, in case it didn't sink in the first time. Did you believe it when you said it? Or did you wonder if you were really worthy of love?

Notice this statement isn't "I am loved, for now" or "I am loved, as long as I make right choices." It's amazing how often we subconsciously add those conditions when we think of God's love for us. Our own love for others tends to be so conditional on their actions toward us that it's difficult to comprehend a love that cannot be defeated. When we aren't lovable, we start worrying we won't be loved. But God's love isn't changeable. It's not contingent on our maturity or even our response. God loved us before we knew he existed. He loved us when we were ignoring him. He loved us when we joined his family but then kept falling back into sin. He loves us now, even though he sees every wrong we've committed and every sin we will be guilty of in the future. His love for us is unbreakable.

Understanding this brings a feeling many of us often don't experience—peace. We don't have to maintain some facade of worthiness or perform at a certain level of holiness in order to keep God's love. We have that love already. And that will never change. God loves us with a love that cannot be broken by outside forces or internal failures.

This confidence comes with a peace that replaces the anxiety and self-condemnation that are so often the soundtracks of our lives.

GOD LOVES US WITH A LOVE THAT
CANNOT BE BROKEN BY OUTSIDE FORCES
OR INTERNAL FAILURES.

God's unbreakable love means we have freedom to learn and grow. And along with that, we have freedom to fail. Just as no child learns to walk without falling or to talk without mispronouncing words in hilarious and adorable ways, so too, we don't grow into who God created us to be without occasionally messing up. Throughout this lifelong process of growth, God's love holds us, protects us, guides us, and picks us back up when we fall.

The strength of his love for us becomes the foundation and the pattern for us to love others. We were created to live in loving relationships with other people, not just God. Loneliness is not our destiny. God is the God who "sets the lonely in families" (Ps. 68:6). His unbreakable love for us gives us the security and peace we need to step into the risks inherent in human relationships. Regardless of how often we mess up in our interactions with others, God's faithful love picks us back up, holds us close, then encourages us to try again.

The strength of his love for us models how we can persevere in loving others even when they are imperfect or weak. Anyone who has been married for longer than about four days knows that the people we love don't act particularly lovable at times. And neither do we. Strong, enduring relationships are grounded in a love that doesn't give up when things get tough. Just as God's love is stronger than our weaknesses and failures, so our own love for others can be strong enough to conquer the obstacles life throws our way.

LOVE IS MESSY People are complicated. We are unpredictable, inconsistent, complex, and ever-changing. As often as we try to put people into the boxes we've made for them, they insist on breaking out. And that means relationships are very messy things indeed.

Movies use this complexity to drive plotlines, but they rarely capture love in all its glorious messiness. It's not their fault—audiences want conflicts resolved and loose ends tied up by the end of the story. We want characters with enough originality to be interesting but enough familiarity to make us comfortable. We want them to fit into our ideas of heroes and villains and sidekicks. Boxes are so satisfying.

Real love, in real life, is endlessly messy. It's glorious and captivating and frustrating and agonizing all at once. It's unpredictable. Uncomfortable. Beyond common sense.

God's essay on love in 1 Corinthians 13 emphasizes this reality through the words and phrases it uses to describe love: patient, kind, humble, and protective. It doesn't get angry easily, doesn't hold grudges, and isn't rude. Why are all those descriptions necessary? Because the people we love will test every single one of those claims—usually before nine o'clock in the morning. The people we love aren't perfect. They are lovable one minute and hateful the next. They, like ourselves, want to do what is right, but regularly fail at it. Love is messy because people are.

God's love embraces this mess. His love is constant, powerful, and dependable. He remains committed to loving us no matter how creatively we sabotage our own lives. We are loved, even when we don't deserve it. The Bible says that "if we are faithless, he remains faithful, for he cannot disown himself" (2 Tim. 2:13). His love for us is grounded in his very nature. It doesn't falter in the face of our failures. It embraces us, messes and all.

God isn't waiting for you to fix yourself before he accepts you. He's not standing outside your life holding a checklist, waiting for you to get yourself together in enough areas before he can tolerate your presence. He loves you now, as you are.

Jesus's story about the prodigal son, found in Luke 15:11–32, gives us a glimpse of how God's love handles the craziness of human relationships. You probably know the story. A young man decides he doesn't want to wait for his father to die and pass on his inheritance; he wants the money now. The father gives him his share, and the son promptly leaves on a road trip with his new riches. It doesn't take long before the party lifestyle leaves him broke and broken. In desperation he hires himself out as a worker on a pig farm.

GOD ISN'T WAITING FOR YOU TO FIX YOURSELF BEFORE HE ACCEPTS YOU.

One morning as he feeds slop to the pigs, he realizes in shock that he is jealous of the pigs, because they have more to eat than he does. He forms a new plan: he'll go home and beg. He knows he's lost his position as son, but he's hopeful he can at least get a job as a servant working for his dad.

So a few days later, the young man—dirty, starving, lonely, and broken—walks down the road toward the home that used to be his. In the distance, standing on the porch, he can see his father staring at him. The son takes a deep breath, getting ready to make his plea for a job. But the words die in his throat as his father dashes up to him and wraps him in a bear hug, ignoring the dust and pig odor and the disapproving stares of the townspeople. In his exuberance the father shouts for his servants, ordering them to bring clean clothes and a ring and to prepare a party in celebration. His son has returned!

This is love, and it's messy. Think about it. The son has been a certifiable jerk. He's dishonored the family. He's lost a lot of money. Accepting this kid back into the family is not going to be as simple as just pretending nothing happened. The older brother makes that clear when he returns home and throws himself a party of his own—a pity party. But the father doesn't care about the complexities or the problems or the obstacles. He just loves his kids, both of them. No matter what.

That's the Father's love for you. For each of us. No matter how badly we screw up, he is waiting for us with a bear hug and a fresh start.

In our human relationships, this ability of love to embrace the messiness of reality is essential. Love is about people. It's about openness. It's being able to be intimate, vulnerable, honest, and imperfect—together. It's scary because there is no guarantee we will stay safe and in control. As author C. S. Lewis put it:

> To love at all is to be vulnerable. Love anything and your heart will be wrung and possibly broken. If you want to make sure of keeping it intact you must give it to no one, not even an animal. Wrap it carefully round with hobbies and little luxuries; avoid all entanglements. Lock it up safe in the casket or coffin of your selfishness. But in that casket, safe, dark, motionless, airless, it will change. It will not be broken; it will become unbreakable, impenetrable, irredeemable. . . . The only place outside Heaven where you can be perfectly safe from all the dangers and per-turbations of love is Hell.[1]

Love is complicated and beautiful, painful and glorious. As we understand just how much God's love embraces us in all our im-perfections, we understand better and better how to extend that graciousness to others around us. We burn the boxes and learn to just embrace the crazy uniqueness of those we love.

LOVE IS COMMITTED Love that can handle the messiness of rela-tionships is love that is committed. It's invested in the success of the relationship and of the other person. As 1 Corinthians 13 says, it "always hopes" and "never fails."

YOU KEEP TRACK OF ALL MY SORROWS. YOU HAVE COLLECTED ALL MY TEARS IN YOUR BOTTLE. YOU HAVE RECORDED EACH ONE IN YOUR BOOK. (PS. 56:8 NLT)

After many years of wandering in the wilderness, I found my way back to the Lord. As the Holy Spirit started transforming my heart, I experienced many, many tears! But I have learned through this season that instead of giving my feelings power over me, or suppressing them and ignoring them, I can simply bring them to my Father, who cares deeply for me. He knows what I am going through and wants to comfort me, heal me, and give me joy!

Because of the cross, Jesus himself knows what it's like to give a cry of desperation. While he was dying on the cross, he cried out in agony, "My God, my God, why have you abandoned me?" (Matt. 27:46 NLT). On the cross, Jesus got the abandonment that we deserved. He understands our desperation, and he will never abandon us. When we understand the depth of his suffering on the cross for us, we'll never cry for ourselves in the same way again.

CARMEN HORAK

When God created us, he went all in. He didn't hedge his bets. He didn't give himself the option of just trying again with a different creation if we failed. When Adam and Eve sinned, God kept loving. Even through punishment, he reassured them that his plan of redemption was already in motion. When God's chosen people, Israel, failed him, he kept loving and leading them. When Jesus's disciples were dense and immature and foolish, he kept working with those guys. When they gave up on him and fled in terror at his arrest, willing to let him die alone, he still gave his life on their behalf. And after his resurrection, he sought the disciples out to reassure them of his love and his commitment to them.

While we may not have fled from Jesus as dramatically as his disciples did, all of us have failed him. Repeatedly. Sometimes spectacularly. And yet, Jesus keeps loving us. He is committed to us, regardless of our failures.

Paul the apostle understood this firsthand. Before he met Jesus, he was famous in the region for his hatred of Christians. He pursued them from city to city, doing his best to get them arrested and even killed. God's love turned that hatred on its head and transformed a killer into a man willing to risk death to preach God's love to anyone who would listen. Paul had this to say about the power, commitment, and tenacity of divine love:

> If God is for us, who can be against us? He who did not spare his own Son, but gave him up for us all—how will he not also, along with him, graciously give us all things? Who will bring any

charge against those whom God has chosen? It is God who justi-
fies. Who then is the one who condemns? No one. Christ Jesus
who died—more than that, who was raised to life—is at the right
hand of God and is also interceding for us. Who shall separate us
from the love of Christ? Shall trouble or hardship or persecution
or famine or nakedness or danger or sword? . . .

No, in all these things we are more than conquerors through
him who loved us. For I am convinced that neither death nor life,
neither angels nor demons, neither the present nor the future,
nor any powers, neither height nor depth, nor anything else in
all creation, will be able to separate us from the love of God that
is in Christ Jesus our Lord. (Rom. 8:31–35, 37–39)

God's love for us does not waver or fail, and it will not be
stopped. Even when we fall short, it achieves its purpose. Even
when we fall short, God's love does not. It holds fast to us and
restores us.

God's love is committed to our success. Most of the time, this
brings incredible comfort and peace. Sometimes, however, it brings
discomfort. And that is part of love as well. God is so committed

GOD'S LOVE FOR US DOES NOT WAVER OR FAIL.

to loving us that he will willingly disrupt our comfortable lives if he knows we need it. He will allow difficult times in order to help us grow into who he has created us to be. Sometimes those trials are caused directly by our own bad choices, while other times it seems like we're doing everything right but things still go wrong. Either way, God uses the hardships we face to make us more like him—a process that in the end will bring us the happiness and peace that is our heart's desire.

We don't like this part of God's love any more than a toddler likes being told no in the candy aisle of the supermarket or a teenager likes getting grounded for practicing their graffiti skills on the side of the neighbor's toolshed. We want to do what *we* want to do, and we are geniuses at justifying our desires to ourselves. God, however, isn't swayed by our persuasive arguments or bullied by our temper tantrums. He is committed to loving us, even when that love means taking us through some difficult experiences for our own good.

Hebrews 12:7 says, "Endure hardship as discipline; God is treating you as his children." While no one in their right mind enjoys being disciplined, it is one of the most loving things God can do for us. If you're going through hardship, don't despair. God is working through it, and he is faithful to guide you and sustain you and to help you to change and grow where it is needed. God is committed to you.

The commitment of love, just like the other aspects of love we've looked at, is essential in human relationships as well. Our love for others must be strong enough that it can survive the inevitable failures of the other person. It can't fall apart the first time one of us messes up.

True love perseveres. There is a reason that marriage ceremonies include vows. When two people get married, they cannot know the future. They have no idea what obstacles or trials they will face. But they are committed to facing those obstacles and those trials together. Love is committed to the success of the other person and of the relationship.

LOVE IS GIVING True love is generous. It is sacrificial, not selfish. It is willing to pay the cost for the relationship to be successful. No friendship or romance will last long if it is primarily selfish. Everything that makes human connection beautiful—honesty, vulnerability, trust, and intimacy—depends on those in the relationship being willing to seek the good of the other person even when that means paying a personal cost.

God's love is a love that constantly gives to us. He gave his Son to die in our place. He gave his Spirit to live inside us and help us. And daily he forgives, strengthens, and encourages. His love isn't for his benefit, but for ours.

As humans, our love for others is usually not this pure. Selfishness runs deep in all of us, so that messiness we talked about earlier often comes into play. But despite how often we might fall short of God's example, we are still made in his image. And we still have the capacity to love others in a way that gives freely and seeks the success of others. Parents do this regularly. Loving small children means losing sleep, privacy, income, and some level of sanity. Relationships with other adults also require a willingness to give. We give each other forgiveness for faults, freedom to express feelings, room to fail, and time to heal.

This does *not* mean that true love allows itself to be victimized by an abuser. Love gives, but it does so for the mutual benefit of those in the relationship, not to enable an abuser to continue manipulating you or anyone else. Love is a choice. If you are in a relationship where that choice has been taken from you, where you are made to feel bad no matter what you do, or where you are doing all the giving while the other person does all the receiving, that is a not a healthy relationship, and you need to seek counsel and change. Love gives, but that giving doesn't take away freedom, self-worth, or choice. The loving and the giving need to go both ways.

GOD'S LOVE WRAPS US IN HIS ARMS, DESPITE THE MESSES WE MAKE, AND CARRIES US INTO THE FUTURE HE HAS PREPARED FOR US.

I am loved. Such a simple yet powerful truth. Even a child can understand it to some extent (in fact, sometimes they understand it better than adults do), but it takes a lifetime and more to fully grasp the depth of its meaning for us. God's love—strong, committed, and giving—wraps us in his arms, despite the messes we make, and carries us into the future he has prepared for us.

I AM LOVED, so I love without reservation. My capacity to give and receive love is beyond measure. I'm protected by the truth that nothing can escape the reach of my Father's love. This eternal love extends beyond the confines of time, connecting every culture, generation, and location. God's perfect love expels all fear, inviting me to love those—including myself—who are "scary" to love. When it's all said and done, I can love others because my Father first loved me. I am loved, *so I love without reservation.*

SECURE

THINK BACK TO YOUR CHILDHOOD for a second. When you were young—so young that maybe now you only have the vaguest memories of that time—there's a good chance you had a special blanket. Or maybe it was a stuffed animal or a toy. Whatever it was, it was inexplicably and undeniably precious to you. You held it close, insisted on sleeping with it, and panicked if you lost it. In that sense, it was the preschool equivalent of your cell phone. That blanket or animal probably had a name, and to you it was more cherished than anything on the planet. Your family could probably tell stories of frantic searches when it went missing, failed attempts at providing substitutes, and the almost magical way you calmed down when it was finally located (or the ear-piercing wails of a lost soul being informed that Bunny hadn't survived its ride down the freeway on the roof of the minivan and was never coming back).

The need for security is a primal desire in all of us. It doesn't go away when we outgrow Blankie or Baba or whatever embarrassing name we gave that magical item. The need stays deep inside us. It drives many of our decisions in life, whether we realize it or not. It pushes us to act or it holds us back. It encourages us to develop relationships, but then makes us reluctant to share too deeply. It drives us to work hard and earn money but cautions us against taking risks. It shapes our responses to others' words and actions in ways we often don't even realize.

The desire to feel secure is universal. It's part of being human. It's normal, understandable, and healthy. We all yearn to know that we are safe, that the world won't harm us, that there is no monster hoping we'll forget to close our closet door so he can have us for his midnight snack.

Security is the sense that we are safe from threats, whether present or future. It is a confidence that we are protected from risk. These risks might be tangible: the threat of physical harm from others or of lacking food or shelter. Or they might be intangible: the risk of failing at something important, of being embarrassed or ridiculed or rejected, the secret terror that we are not adequate for the task in front of us and will inevitably be outed as imposters.

Psychologist Abraham Maslow, in his famous "hierarchy of needs," theorized that after basic physical needs such as air, food, and water are met, the most fundamental human need is that of safety.[1] His theories have been foundational to modern psychology in part because they ring true with our experience. We *need* to feel secure and safe in order to be truly whole.

WE NEED TO FEEL SECURE AND SAFE IN ORDER TO BE TRULY WHOLE.

As we grew up, part of the emotional minefield of elementary and middle school was the uncomfortable realization of how big and powerful and uncontrollable the world really is. Add to that our society's constant push to experience everything, to excel at everything, and to win at everything, and somewhere deep inside, we start wishing we could just go back to that time when our security blanket was the answer to all our problems.

Of course, no blanket can shield us from adulthood and the risks that come with growing up. When we recognize these risks but don't have an answer for how to protect ourselves from them, we end up with chronic anxiety. Anxiety has become a defining characteristic of youth. Studies in the early 2000s determined that teenagers in the 1980s had average anxiety levels as high as those of psychiatric patients in the 1950s. If anything, the severity of the problem has only increased since then.[2] And if our own internal fears aren't enough, the internet provides us with instant access to all the world's problems. Climate change, racial tensions, job insecurity, crime rates, pandemics, increasingly unaffordable housing and health care—there seems to be a new disaster on the horizon every time we check the news.

SECURITY VS. CONTROL Our instinctive reaction to this sense of insecurity is to frantically work to eliminate risks. Seems logical, doesn't it? We will be safe when everything that threatens us has been destroyed, or at least removed so far from us that it can no longer touch us. We just need to make our lives a castle, protected from all enemies by our strong position and hard work. The answer to insecurity, we think, is to get rid of anything unknown or dangerous.

Well, no. We wish we could guarantee our security by working hard enough at it that we could control our own destiny, make our own reality, and choose our own adventure. That sounds enticing since it puts us in charge. Because when we're truly honest with ourselves, our desire to be secure often means a desire to be *in control*.

The desire to be secure is a wise and healthy one. The compulsive need to be in control . . . not so much. The need for control, more often than not, reveals that at some subtle, even subconscious level, we believe we can only really depend on ourselves in this life.

Now don't get us wrong. God has made us in his image, and that includes the power to make choices, to control ourselves, and to influence others. We're not saying the key to feeling secure is to simply curl up in bed and binge Netflix while waiting for God to drag you and your weighted blanket toward your destiny. But we are suggesting that we need to separate security (the sense of being safe) from control (the need to save yourself).

As sons and daughters of God, we have a security that the world can only yearn for: the most powerful force in the universe is our Father, our friend, and our defender.

FACING THE SEA We put ourselves through unnecessary agony when we forget how faithful God is in the storms of life. If you've ever read the Old Testament stories about the Israelites' journey from Egypt to the promised land, you've probably rolled your eyes at how dumb those people were. They had front-row seats as God set one creative plague after another on the Egyptians. Rivers turning to blood, a frog invasion, a gnat invasion, a fly invasion, killer hail . . . it just went on and on. If memes had been a thing back then, that year would have produced some amazing ones, complete with hieroglyph-inspired emojis. But despite seeing God's awesome power and protection firsthand, the Israelites never really trusted him. Time after time, when danger threatened them or life didn't

AS SONS AND DAUGHTERS OF GOD, WE HAVE A SECURITY THAT THE WORLD CAN ONLY YEARN FOR.

go the way they wanted, they assumed God had abandoned them. Reading the stories, it's easy to shake our heads at their lack of trust, their unfounded fears, and their constant assumptions that God's protection wouldn't be enough.

Then we find ourselves standing in front of our own Red Sea. Student loan debt, a bad job market, health problems, or any of a thousand other seemingly deadly obstacles defy us, and we quickly find out just how much like the Israelites we really are. And while we might be embarrassed by how weak our trust in God proves to be when it's our own life on the line, these experiences are helping us learn to live in the security and confidence that are our birthright.

Maybe you've known about God's strength and his love for you since the days when your greatest trial in life was being forced to eat carrot sticks when what you *really* wanted was gummy bears. Or maybe your relationship with God began more recently, and you're understanding more each day how powerful and present he is. Either way, we all know God can protect us. We've heard it, we've sung it, we've prayed it, maybe we've even preached it. But when push comes to shove, and our personal Egyptian army is breathing down our backs, it's shockingly difficult to really *live* it.

So we get anxious, worried, and afraid. Then we feel guilty for being anxious, and we worry that our anxiety is a lack of faith and that our unbelief will keep God from helping us. So then we feel more anxious about our excessive worry. And that makes us feel even more guilty . . . and the cycle goes on and on and on until we want to curl up in a fetal position and wait for the world to end.

If that's you, we have some good news. God isn't nearly as offended by your humanness as you might think. You're not an intern in a company run by God, trying to prove your worth so you can get a permanent position. You are a child, with a position in the family that cannot be taken from you. Yes, you have a part to play in God's plan, and that part will require courage. Yes, God's desire for you is to live in security and confidence rather than fear. But that lesson is one learned over time by facing trials and seeing God's continued faithfulness. Your current failures, immaturity, weaknesses, or fears don't disappoint your Father. He isn't ashamed of you, even if you are ashamed of yourself. He's deeply, irrevocably, unbelievably in love with you. And because he loves you, he is committed to helping you grow in security.

That sometimes means leading you right up to an impossible ocean of difficulties with an army (a metaphorical one, hopefully) on your tail. God wants to show you something: he is just as powerful now as he has ever been. He's just as committed to

OUR SECURITY IS NOT FOUND IN OUR ABILITY TO CONTROL OUR LIVES. IT IS FOUND IN GOD HIMSELF.

you as he was to his people during the days of Moses. He's still your rock, still your fortress, still your refuge, and still your way through the waters.

Our security is not found in our ability to control our lives. It is found in God himself. That's why Paul, who lived one of the most unsafe lives you can imagine, was able to say triumphantly, "If God is for us, who can be against us?" (Rom. 8:31). He knew that true safety is found not in avoidance of risk but in the all-powerful arms of God. It's why David could face Goliath on the battlefield, why he could stay mentally and emotionally strong while being hunted by Saul, and why he could handle the pressures and fears of running an entire kingdom. And it's why we can face threats, risks, and even pain unbowed, knowing that we are not called to save ourselves but to trust in the God who saves us.

PROMISES If the source of our security is God's power and his committed love for us, then the pathway to feeling secure is understanding his promises in this area. Here are a few of those promises, although there are many more.

God Is with Us Always In the garden of Eden, God walked with Adam and Eve. He spent time with them, as friends would, just hanging out. Not to demand worship or action but to enjoy their presence. Sin broke that relationship, but God sent Jesus to restore it. One of the names Jesus was given was Emmanuel,

MAKES SENSE AND WHAT FEELS LIKE A TANGIBLE DARKNESS SURROUNDS US, WHERE WE DON'T KNOW WHAT
TO STAY STRONG OURSELVES, MUCH LESS ENCOURAGE OTHERS TO DO SO. THE DARKNESS SEEMS TOO TERRIFYING. I THINK EVERY ONE OF US HAS GONE T
HAT FEELS LIKE A TANGIBLE DARKNESS SURROUNDS US, WHERE WE DON'T KNOW WHAT'S GOING TO HAPPEN AND ARE TERRIFIED BY THAT. IN THOSE TIM
MUCH LESS ENCOURAGE OTHERS TO DO SO. THE DARKNESS SEEMS TOO TERRIFYING. I THINK EVERY ONE OF US HAS GONE THROUGH SEASONS WHERE NO
TERRIFIED BY THAT. IN THOSE TIMES IT CAN SEEM NEARLY IMPOS

I THINK EVERY ONE OF US HAS GONE THROUGH SEASONS WHERE NOTHING MAKES SENSE AND WHAT FEELS LIKE A TANGIBLE DARKNESS SURROUNDS US, WHERE WE DON'T KNOW WHAT'S GOING TO HAPPEN AND ARE TERRIFIED BY THAT. IN THOSE TIMES IT CAN SEEM NEARLY IMPOSSIBLE TO STAY STRONG OURSELVES, MUCH LESS ENCOURAGE OTHERS TO DO SO. THE DARKNESS SEEMS TOO TERRIFYING.

And yet, we see in the Bible that God himself dealt with the darkness. How? In Genesis 1:5, he named the darkness night!

You might wonder, what's the difference?

Well, you see, darkness *suggests endlessness and perpetuity, while* night *is a specific and limited time period. Night eventually turns into something beautiful and full of hope, peace, rest, and mercy. It becomes morning. Whatever the darkness surrounding you—pain, brokenness, disease, loss, hurt, or loneliness—God is whispering, "It's just a night."*

LE IMPOSSIBLE TO STAY S
GE AND WHAT FEELS LIKE A TANGIBLE DARKNESS SURROUNDS US, WHERE WE DON'T KNOW WHAT'S GOING TO HAPPEN AND ARE TERRIFIED BY THAT. IN
OURSELVES, MUCH LESS ENCOURAGE OTHERS TO DO SO. THE DARKNESS SEEMS TOO TERRIFYING. I THINK EVERY ONE OF US HAS GONE THROUGH SEASON
IBLE DARKNESS SURROUNDS US, WHERE WE DON'T KNOW WHAT'S GOING TO HAPPEN AND ARE TERRIFIED BY THAT. IN THOSE TIMES IT CAN SEEM
COURAGE OTHERS TO DO SO. THE DARKNESS SEEMS TOO TERRIFYING. I THINK EVERY ONE OF US HAS GONE THROUGH SEASONS WHERE NOTHING MAKES SE
WHERE WE DON'T KNOW WHAT'S GOING TO HAPPEN AND ARE TERRIFIED BY THAT. IN THOSE TIMES IT CAN SEEM NEARLY IMPOSSIBLE TO STAY STRONG
TERRIFYING. I THINK EVERY ONE OF US HAS GONE THROUGH SEASONS WHERE NOTHING MAKES SENSE AND WHAT FEELS LIKE A TANGI
LESS ENCOUR

There's a joy beyond your bitter tears; darkness will not endure forever. "Weeping may last through the night, but joy comes with the morning" (Ps. 30:5 NLT). So wait on the Lord, and wait for the dawn. "Be strong and take heart and wait for the LORD" (Ps. 27:14). This is just a night, and as God ordered, the morning shall surely follow.

MARIAN STEPANYAN

which literally means "God with us." He left heaven in order to restore us to an intimate relationship with his Father, who had never given up on his people. No other religion or philosophy has the audacity to suggest that divine love could extend this far. It's mind-blowing to think that God values us—not our service, not our obedience, but *us*—to that degree. And before Jesus returned to heaven, he promised that his Holy Spirit would come to live in us. Whether we realize it or not, God himself has taken up residence inside of us, not to control us but to encourage and strengthen us. God promises that his presence will never leave us alone.

God Is for Us   God isn't just with us, he's *for* us. That's an important distinction. God is not merely a witness of what we do or don't do, a passive watcher along for the ride. He's not a coldhearted, disengaged judge whose only goal is to point out our mistakes and decree punishment. God is actively, intimately involved in helping us live out the life he's called us to have. Philippians 2:13 says, "For God is working in you, giving you the desire and the power to do what pleases him" (NLT). That desire we feel inside to do what is right comes from God. And the ability to do it comes from the same source. Of all the possible allies we could have in this universe, we have God himself. It doesn't get better than that.

God Forgives Us   For many Christians, one of our greatest sources of insecurity is the nagging feeling that we aren't "good enough."

We know our sins, even the secret ones that others can't see. We've read the Bible, and we know we don't measure up. Not even close. Sure, everyone else has sinned too, and God forgives them. But our sin is special. It's bigger. It's badder. It's too shameful for God to fully absolve.

This, of course, makes no sense. Shame rarely does. But that doesn't stop Satan from using it with remarkable effectiveness.

The Bible is clear that God has forgiven us. All of us, including you and me. Psalm 103:12 declares, "As far as the east is from the west, so far has he removed our transgressions from us." And Romans 8:1 reassures us, "There is therefore now no condemnation for those who are in Christ Jesus" (ESV). Like every other promise of God, though, it seems too good, too free, to be true. Surely we deserve some punishment.

On the one hand, it's healthy to feel sorrow for our sins. That's part of repentance. It helps motivate us to actually change. But Satan loves to wait for us to sin, then he piles on condemnation, guilt, and shame in order to bury us in hopelessness and self-loathing. He'd love to convince us that God's forgiveness is limited, like a coupon that can only be used for a limited time or a Monopoly "Get Out of Jail Free" card that has to be turned in once used.

God's forgiveness isn't limited. It doesn't expire, get old, or get revoked. We don't have to come cringing before God each time we've screwed up, terrified that this time is the last straw. Instead, we "come boldly to the throne of our gracious God" (Heb. 4:16

NLT), because we are not trusting in our own righteousness but in the incredible, unlimited grace of our Father.

God Provides for Us   We humans are needy. We need air, water, food, clothing, shelter, relationships, and regular doses of caffeine (yes, that last one is a need for some of us—don't be so judgmental). So when the Bible promises that "God will meet all your needs according to the riches of his glory in Christ Jesus" (Phil. 4:19), that is good news indeed. Read that promise again, because every word matters.

> God isn't just God; he's *my* God, he's *our* God.
>
> He doesn't just meet a few of our needs; he meets *all* of them.
>
> He doesn't just barely meet our needs; he opens the windows of heaven and rains down *glorious riches*.
>
> And he doesn't give us those riches based on what we deserve (imagine how well that would work out for most of us!) but on the finished work of *Jesus Christ*.

OUR FATHER KNOWS OUR NEEDS— EVEN THE ONES WE DON'T SEE OURSELVES.

If we really grasp this, then it's nearly impossible to fear the future. As God's children, we receive his provision. That promise is based on our relationship with him, not our performance. Of course, this doesn't mean we get to demand everything we want, like spoiled children manipulating their parents into meeting their every whim. It doesn't mean we have God's blessing to spend every dollar of our paycheck on video games or late-night online shopping sprees and expect Visa to send the bill straight to heaven.

But it does mean our Father knows our needs—even the ones we don't see ourselves—and he has promised to employ the power of heaven itself to meet them. It means we don't have to madly pursue worldly success in order to be secure from troubles that might come. The author of Hebrews put it this way: "Keep your lives free from the love of money and be content with what you have, because God has said, 'Never will I leave you; never will I forsake you.' So we say with confidence, 'The Lord is my helper; I will not be afraid. What can mere mortals do to me?'" (13:5–6).

This promise is particularly crucial because the topic of provision, or finances, is one of the most common training grounds God uses to help us become more secure in him. It is easy to say we trust God. But then we get laid off or become too sick to work or find ourselves responsible for meeting not only our own needs but those of our spouse and children on an income that seems impossibly small. During these times of trial, God's promises can seem far-fetched, unrealistic, and unlikely. It doesn't help, of course, that we often sabotage ourselves with poor spending

One night I went to a leader meeting. I tried to engage in the worship service, but the condemning thoughts dominated the entire time of worship. The message the speakers shared was simple but powerful: Don't be so busy for God that you get too busy to be with God.

That basically summed up my whole summer. At the end of the message, I went to a corner of the room to pray.

When I went to that corner, God was waiting. It felt like there had been an appointment set in heaven, and while I had been unaware of it, God was not going to miss it. He had come to meet me, even if I didn't deserve it. His presence was tangible.

I started telling God how sorry I was for my failures. Then I stopped, and just asked, "Lord, what pleases you the most?" I heard him reply, "Let me love you." I started to go on apologizing again for how bad I was, but he interrupted. "Let me love you!" His words were so passionate, like he was crying out for me to allow him to love me. I saw a picture of him trying to come close and embrace me, but I had my arms up resisting him and trying to keep him at arm's length with all my excuses for why I didn't deserve his love. But his intensity, pursuit, and passion would not give up. "Let me love you! Let me love you! Let me love you!"

Finally, I surrendered. At that moment it felt like he picked me up and embraced me as his son. There really are no words to describe the intensity of the experience. I've heard the human body has thirty trillion cells—it was like his love was wrapped around every last one of mine. Every fiber of my being was immersed in his love for me. I wept and wept as he kept showing me how much he loves me.

That encounter changed my life forever. The guilt, condemnation, and sin I was dealing with in that season lost its grip on me. God is passionate about me—and about you. He wants to show you how much he loves you, in whatever way you need to receive it.

DAVID GUTIERREZ

or savings habits. Between our mistakes and the cruel blows of fate, we can find ourselves with our backs to the wall and no solution in sight.

That is where trust grows. As we stand on the promises of God, and as we listen to his voice telling us what to do, we begin to learn real trust. All the study in the world is no substitute in this area for personal experience. God does provide. Not just for Saints in the Bible. Not just for your pastor. Not just for holy people you know. He provides for you. Stand on that truth. Believe it. Wait for it if necessary. Be willing to make the changes in your lifestyle that he's leading you to make, and we promise you, you will see his faithfulness. He provides for his children.

God Protects Us Contrary to what some people seem to think about God, his most often-repeated command in the Bible is not "do not sin" or "do not have fun." It is "do not be afraid." Fear does have its place in this world. If you're strolling across a road and suddenly see a truck bearing down on you, fear is probably a more helpful emotion in the moment than happiness or content- ment. But it's not meant to be a constant state of mind for God's sons and daughters. We don't have to fear the future. God has promised to protect us. There are literally dozens of Bible verses stating this (Psalm 91 alone has many), not to mention all the Bible stories where heroes of the faith are miraculously rescued by God. God keeps us safe from harm.

NOTHING IN THE UNIVERSE CAN DERAIL GOD'S PURPOSES.

Except when he doesn't. The promises can start ringing a little hollow when real life slams into our Sunday school theology. Because let's be honest with ourselves, Christians still get hurt. Christians get cancer, lose their jobs, suffer domestic abuse, get robbed and raped and murdered. Those who have a healthy family and live in a relatively stable or prosperous country might get away with living in a bubble for a while, freely ignoring how savage life can really be. But sooner or later, we all deal with the reality of pain.

These conversations sometimes make Christians uncomfortable. We don't want to admit that a loving Father could allow his children to hurt—especially when we are those children! But the Bible doesn't share our squeamishness. Many of the heroes of faith endured incredible suffering, including the very ones writing the promises about God's protection. God's promises in his Word were not written by people oblivious to the existence of evil but people who knew God's power to triumph over it.

IT NEVER ENDS So how do we stand secure in God's promises? First, we need to recognize that no sin of ours or others, no evil twist of fate, nothing in the universe, can derail God's purposes. He doesn't need a backup plan. He is sovereign over this universe. Yes, humans make choices, and some of those choices are incredibly stupid and harmful. But God is bigger than our messes. He really does work everything together for the good of his children, even if we don't see it yet.

Second, we need to recognize that our actual life span is eternity itself. When our lives are going well, we tend to think very little about eternity. But when terminal cancer strikes a loved one or we are the victim of a violent crime or some other crisis crashes into our life like a meteorite of pain, we come face-to-face with the grim reality of life on a fallen planet. We begin to realize why so much of the New Testament talks about heaven. Converts to Christianity in the early days of the church faced intense persecution—loss of property, jobs, status, freedom, and sometimes life. Their view of God's protection was a little more balanced than ours sometimes is. They recognized that God could save them, but if he chose not to do so, they immediately inherited heaven. Either way was a win.

It still is. The world is fixated on living longer, healthier, richer lives because that's all they have to look forward to—death is seen as the end. But for us, it's just the beginning. It's a safe bet that no one in heaven is sad when they arrive.

These promises of God—that he is with us, that he is for us, that he forgives us, that he provides for us, and that he protects us—are a foundation on which to stand and face the uncertainties of life. We can't control every aspect of our lives, no matter how hard we try. But we don't have to. We'd mess it up anyway, more than likely. Instead, we can do our best to live wisely and passionately, knowing our confidence rests in our Father's power and love for us. No matter what storm is brewing on the horizon, we know we are safe. We can say with confidence, "I am secure. My Father is watching out for me."

I AM SECURE, so I live from a place of peace. A life of peace is my inheritance. It's part of my family legacy. I live knowing that peace isn't found in having all the answers—it comes from being in tune with the One who has all the answers. In my Father, I am secure. His Spirit wraps me in eternal promises. He orders my steps and fills my life with unexpected brilliance. There's joy in knowing that my future is greater than what I can see in this moment. My life is bigger than what I can build with my hands. I am secure, *so I live from a place of peace.*

I AM

CONFIDENT

IF YOU'VE EVER PREPARED for a job interview, chances are you sought advice from the infallible internet. There, thousands of blog writers compete to offer their best tips on the topic. Set aside for a second the unsettling question, If their advice is so good, why have they resorted to writing free blogs on the internet? and look at what they have to say. While there are plenty of conflicting opinions on how to land your dream job, one word shows up over and over again in these articles: *confidence*. This mysterious quality will supposedly help you impress the interviewer, land your dream job, and negotiate a killer salary. Dating sites give similar advice, promising that men are more attracted to confident women and vice versa. In fact, the promise that we will feel more confident if we buy some product is used to sell everything from questionable diets to adult diapers.

When we think of a confident person, most of us probably picture a man or woman standing tall, chin up, with their eyes fearlessly focused on their goal. Their clothing is sharp and stylish, and they smell of success. If they *are* wearing adult diapers, no one will ever find out. They know what they want, and they know that they have what it takes to get it. Everyone in their world is attracted to them because they seem so, well, confident.

Faced with the realization of how important confidence is to succeed in life, many of us look deep inside ourselves. And we panic. We aren't confident. We aren't bold. We can sometimes fake it with enough caffeine and desperation, but we don't feel nearly as confident as we are told we *ought* to be. So we pretend. We stand taller and force ourselves to make eye contact, and we shake hands with a nice firm grip that hopefully isn't dripping with nervous sweat. "Fake it till you make it" becomes our mantra.

We rarely stop to wonder how many of the apparently confident people around us are giving themselves the same pep talk. Instead, we assume we are the imposters in the group. We are the ones whose incompetence will soon be the talk of the town. Everyone else is totally sure of themselves and not faking anything, right?

Wrong. Appearing confident is easier than being confident, and plenty of people are scared spitless behind their self-assured facade. That doesn't mean we assume people are faking their confidence, but let's not assume they are demigods either.

Some people mistake arrogance for confidence. They are convinced that they are smarter than everyone around and that the world is not worthy of their presence. But this isn't true confidence

APPEARING CONFIDENT IS EASIER THAN BEING CONFIDENT.

any more than the fake confidence we just mentioned. Neither "I'm an imposter" nor "I'm God's greatest gift to humankind" is the voice of real confidence. Both are counterfeits.

God offers the real thing. Real confidence can be defined as "an awareness of who you are, regardless of how you compare or measure up to others."[1] It is born out of an inner security that doesn't need constant affirmation from others, that doesn't have to dominate to prove itself, that isn't shaken by failure because it wasn't built on performance in the first place. That inner security is what we discussed in the last chapter. As sons and daughters of God, created and loved and cared for by him, we have a security that nothing can shake. That inner sense of knowing who we are and what we are worth in God's eyes is what enables us to be really confident.

Confidence is how we feel and act once we grasp what Jesus has done to make us holy, righteous, loved, and secure. If security is the inner peace of understanding our worth, then confidence is the outward expression of that security.

True confidence can't be faked, at least not for long. In times of conflict, uncertainty, or failure, our core beliefs are revealed. And since these things are near-daily companions in this crazy journey we call life, who we are will eventually come out. If our confidence is merely a facade, it will crack. If our confidence is just pride in our supposedly superior abilities, it will crumble. But if our confidence is the authentic outward expression of an unshakable inner security in Christ, we will stand.

Unlike fake confidence or arrogance, true confidence is able to be both bold and humble, strong and gentle, assertive and supportive, wise and teachable. Let's look at each of these in a little more detail.

HUMBLE BOLDNESS   Boldness is the willingness to take initiative to achieve something risky or uncertain. It is easy to see how boldness relates to confidence: bold people are confident that they can achieve the goal they are aiming for, even when others are too scared of the risks to even try. What we don't often realize is that true, godly confidence also produces humility. And humility makes boldness far more effective.

BOLDNESS WITHOUT HUMILITY IS NOTHING BUT ARROGANCE.

BOLDNESS WITH HUMILITY GIVES US THE FREEDOM TO FAIL.

Boldness *without* humility is nothing but arrogance. It thrives on ignorance and denial, refusing to admit the possibility of failure. It can produce great things because it motivates us to take the risks necessary to bring great results. But on its own, it is an uncontrolled flame, a disaster waiting to happen. Boldness unconstrained by humility rarely admits need, danger, or failure. It pushes us to take on tasks that we shouldn't, carry burdens that aren't ours, muddle through and make a mess of things rather than ask for help, and incur risks that wisdom would have avoided.

Boldness *with* humility gives us the freedom to fail, the honesty to admit when we don't have the answers, and the ability to ask for help when we need it. It takes real courage to be humble—a lot more courage than to just brag and bluster our way through life. The confidence that comes from God allows us to be humble and that adds strength and balance to the boldness.

We are indeed attracted to confident people. But that is not just because they seem to have the answers. In fact, if someone does have all the answers, we typically find them annoying! Confident people know when they know something, but they also know when they don't, and they are humble enough to say it. That honesty endears them to other people. And that is exactly the kind of confidence that God instills in us as we walk in his ways.

GENTLE STRENGTH Cultures throughout human history have glorified strength. Military conquests, duels, sporting events, even our economic system of capitalism—all of them reward the strong. "To the victor belong the spoils" and "survival of the fittest" have become truisms in our society. And this brash, visible strength is often connected with confidence. We assume that strong people are confident, and confident people are strong.

There is a connection between the two, but it might not be what you think. Strength can actually be a display not of confidence but of insecurity, of ego, of fear. It can be a result of unchecked selfishness and near sociopathic disregard for the needs of others. Dictators and oppressive regimes have committed unspeakable atrocities simply because they had the power to get what they wanted and didn't care whom they hurt to get it.

The confidence God has for us is strong, but it's not brutal or self-serving. True strength is power under control. What good are strong arms if they lack the muscle control to pick up a glass without crushing it or hold a child without hurting her? True strength is gentle. It can do what needs to be done, but it avoids harming others in the process.

Gentle strength is directly connected to our confidence. It is what allows us to be careful, humble, and self-controlled.

ANCE, I'M LEARNING TO WHOLEHEARTEDLY TRUST IN HIS LEADING, TRUST IN HIS EVERY MOVE, EVERY STEP, EVERY TURN, AND EVERY DIP. NG, TRUST IN HIS EVERY MOVE, EVERY STEP, EVERY TURN, AND EVERY DIP. LIKE A DANCE, I'M LEARNING TO WHOLEHEARTEDLY TRUST IN HIS LEADING, TRUST IN HIS EVE EVERY DIP. LIKE A DANCE, I'M LEARNING TO WHOLEHEARTEDLY TRUST IN HIS LEADING, TRUST IN HIS EVERY MOVE, EVERY STEP, EVERY TURN, AND EVERY DIP. LIKE A DAN BUST IN HIS LEADING, TRUST IN HIS EVERY MOVE, EVERY STEP, EVERY TURN, AND EVERY DIP. LIKE A DANCE, I'M LEARNING TO WHOLEHEARTEDLY TRUST IN HIS LEADING, TRUST IN HIS EVERY MOVE, EVERY STEP, EVERY TURN, AND EVERY

ONE OF MY BIGGEST WEAKNESSES USED TO BE MY HESITANCY TO CHANGE, ESPECIALLY IF THAT INVOLVED A BIG LEAP OF FAITH. I WAS—OR THOUGHT I WAS— SOMEONE WHO SIMPLY WANTED GOD TO SEND OVER A CLEAR BLUEPRINT AND OUTLINE FOR MY LIFE.

Ironically, when that happened and someone did share what they felt God wanted me to do, it didn't bring peace at all. They shared their dream of how I would share the love of God through dance in untouched places. They said that's where I would find my greatest joy. But all I heard were the personal sacrifices I had to be willing to make. I was confused, doubtful, and skeptical—I wondered why God was opening a door I thought he closed. I found myself saying to God, "It's so hard to trust you when you take the things I hold dear away. It's hard to continue to walk blind."

I wanted to do God's will, but I didn't know if that included the creative ministry I was helping pioneer at that time or this dream of using dance to share the love of God in places I've never been. I reached a fork in the road, and my mind was overwhelmed. I found myself falling down a slippery slope, focused on what I would be losing. A friend challenged me to pray about it and encouraged me with Proverbs 3:5–6, which says that as we lean on and trust God, he will make our paths straight. I didn't have to know the timing of everything or depend on my own understanding, I just needed to submit to God and trust him—to confidently say, "God is enough."

Like a dance, I'm learning to wholeheartedly trust in his leading, trust in his every move, every step, every turn, and every dip. To be close to him—clenching tightly to his hand and letting him hold me and make me feel secure—makes it easier to face change. Learning these truths was—and still is—a process, but I can find security in his character and in his promises, always.

IRA MAMBA

TRUE STRENGTH IS POWER UNDER CONTROL.

To better understand this, think about what a lack of confidence looks like. If we feel threatened, a primal instinct we share with animals kicks in: the fight-or-flight response. When attacked, an animal will by instinct tend toward one of these two responses. Even a pet may run in terror or bite their owner if they are caught off guard and feel threatened.

Humans aren't that different. While we can control our responses, our gut still pushes us instinctively to fight or flee when danger threatens. Obviously, this shouldn't result in you running and screaming down the office hallway or biting your boss if he reprimands you for something. We have more civilized ways to express ourselves—hopefully, at least. But the point is, insecurity or feelings of danger will alter our responses and push them toward unhealthy extremes. Neither fleeing in terror nor fighting for survival are particularly gentle reactions. So if we lack confidence or feel continually in danger, we will be as unpredictable as a terrified animal. We will run away from conflict or shut conversations down or attack those who try to help us with constructive criticism or lash out emotionally or any number of dysfunctional responses.

Confidence stops these extreme reactions before they start. It helps us feel less threatened and more secure. Instead of lashing out in an instinctive fight for survival, we can deal with other people—even when conflict looms—with gentle strength.

STRONG SUPPORT Confidence in our own self-worth and God's love for us is essential to help us walk one of the most difficult tight-ropes of modern-day existence: caring both for ourselves and for those we love. Those two are often in tension. Depending on our personality and how we were raised, we are likely to sacrifice one for the sake of the other. Either we focus on our own needs and desires, despite the need around us, or we become living martyrs and help others, even as our own needs go unmet. Neither of those is healthy, obviously, but it's amazing how often we still fall off one side of the tightrope or the other.

Some people are so focused on their own wants, needs, dreams, and desires that they ignore the needs of those around them. They are selfish or simply oblivious. We have all known people like this, and if we are being honest, we've probably acted this way ourselves quite a few times. It is possible to get so focused on ourselves that we ignore God's command to "share each other's burdens, and in this way obey the law of Christ" (Gal. 6:2 NLT). This is why understanding the true nature of love is essential to living the life God has designed for us (and why you ought to go back and read that love chapter if you skipped it).

But for many of us, the tendency is to fall off the tightrope on the other side. We see the needs of others more clearly than our own. And as Christians, the pressure to put others' needs first is especially strong because we are taught to love others sacrificially, faithfully, and continually. Love involves sacrifice, but that doesn't mean you should ignore your own needs. The people you serve are loved by God, and so are you. They are of infinite worth, and so are you. They have needs, and so do you. You do no one a favor by slowly killing yourself in the name of love.

There are a number of reasons we might help others while ignoring legitimate needs of our own. Maybe we do it because deep inside we believe we aren't worth as much as others. Or we have a gnawing hunger to be appreciated, loved, and valued. We crave the affirmation that comes from being the hero, and we are willing to harm ourselves to get it. Maybe we are scared to displease or anger those who are expecting our help. Or maybe we were taught as children that it is wrong to talk about our needs. An essential part of growing in Christ, however, is gaining the security and confidence to see our own needs, to value them appropriately, and to take necessary steps to meet them.

As we've discussed, the basic human needs are food, air, water, shelter, and safety. Beyond those we need love. We need rest. We need time with people, and we need time alone. We need times of fun, and we need fulfilling work. How much of each of these is needed and how they will actually look in practice depends on the individual. Some of us really enjoy people but primarily in small groups or for short periods of time. Then we just want to curl up with our cat. Others thrive on interactions with lots of people and tend to scare cats. Some of us need eight or nine hours of sleep a night to function well. Others seem to do just fine with six or seven and a lot of coffee.

It is vital that we understand these aren't just selfish desires. They are legitimate needs. And these needs can typically be ignored for only a short while before life becomes increasingly unhealthy. And yet, we often do just that. Because of insecurity, fear, wrong values, or bad teaching, we ignore some needs completely and pretend they aren't real. But those needs do not go away, and they shouldn't. God created us to need those things and wants us to learn to meet them in a way that honors him and brings delight to our lives.

Earlier we quoted Galatians 6:2: "Share each other's burdens, and in this way obey the law of Christ" (NLT). But three verses later we read, "Each one should carry their own load." These verses aren't contradictory but complementary. We are responsible for managing our own responsibilities, but we also need help from others at times. We are not made to live as freeloaders, sponging off the hard work of others. Rather, we are meant to live in community, and we can, and should, both give and receive help when that is needed.

Godly confidence helps us learn to be both assertive and supportive in meeting needs. *Assertive* in this case means that we acknowledge the existence and the validity of our own needs. There will never be a lack of people around us who are eager to accept and even demand our help. If we continue to give, they will continue to take. It's tempting to blame this on them, but that's not where we should be pointing our finger. The responsibility to set appropriate boundaries lies with us. We can and must know when to say, "I'm sorry, but I can't take on that responsibility."

This can be terrifying, as it risks the displeasure of people we love (or, at least, those we are trying to impress), but it is an essential

GODLY CONFIDENCE HELPS US LEARN TO BE BOTH ASSERTIVE AND SUPPORTIVE IN MEETING NEEDS.

part of being healthy. God's desire for us is that we would learn to put appropriate boundaries in place so we can be physically, emotionally, mentally, and spiritually strong. Yes, there will be emergencies where you have to be flexible and set aside your desires and even your needs for a short period. But real emergencies are few and far between (unless you have a toddler, in which case, sometimes they seem to happen daily).

Supportive means that we help others. Caring for our own needs and caring for the needs of others doesn't need to be an either/or choice. True confidence enables us to reach out to others in need and help them—not because we need the affirmation or because we are scared of their disapproval but because we care about them.

When our internal needs are met, we are in a better position to help others. If you've ever been on a plane, you've heard the flight attendant talk about what to do in an emergency. Among lots of other advice, they always tell you that if oxygen masks fall from the ceiling, you should put your own on before you help others. That's not selfishness; it's wisdom. If you try to help someone else while you're dying, it's unlikely to end well for either of you.

I'M NOT A LEADER, PROFOUND SPEAKER, THINKER, OR EVEN AN INVENTOR OF MUCH.

Count me out as a cook, maid, or anything that requires
  great touch.
A scientist I'll never be, not smart enough, No, not me.
An athlete? Please, skilled at what . . . just to live and
  breathe.
All I do is exist, so why do you need me?

All that I thought I could be, seems like a passing dream
  after all of my life's tragedy.
But this book, old and raggedy, yet still remains, keeps
  shouting out at me . . . In my darkest of days.
Give. Me. A. Chance. It says . . . There is still some . . . Wait!
I can't trust your saying. But then again, can my life be
  fixed? Be put back, pieced, glued . . . anything to make
  new . . . if I let you in. You're my last chance, ride, bet,
  ticket to somewhere.

But . . . what am I saying? These old myths, fairy tales,
  this perception of a hero, your "Good News" . . . this
  can't be different, right? They are all the same, told to
  all and criticized and blamed . . . feeding into society's
  hunger for something to look at as sane, positive . . .
  or even a victor over evil.

But, oh . . . I have nothing left.
I have no other alternative, this has to work.

So despite what they say, I open this book and my heart
starts to jerk . . . UP . . . DOWN. Pound!
I fall on the ground, as I read of your Love. Your Amazing
Love!
That . . . that . . . that seems to strike me as foreign, for who
could ever love something,
SOMEONE with its faults slathered all upon them?
But You did. Your son did. He took my pain, my inadequacies,
failures, it all.
And nailed them to a tree cut out to hold all of our iniquities.

I can't believe it . . . but I believe!
In this Gospel, this Man . . . No, My God . . . No! . . .
My Savior. Yes, that is what He is to me.
He found a grain of worth . . . a purpose I was made for. If
to speak of nothing else . . . it was to be made for Him.
Know Him . . . and make Him known.
I have found my calling . . . and it came through a word.
This Word shouts out to everyone here. . . . Hoping you'll
receive it and trust in its value and worth. This Word is
one of many definitions of my Savior, but rings brightest
for ME. . . . This word is HOPE.

Hope to believe that we are here for an unquestion-
able Destiny. That the trials we face are so much
more than pain but what if . . .
to raise our character and Integrity. Hope will raise us up
. . . if rooted in the One who never gives up. . . . On us.
Hope, though not stronger than Love . . . spurs us on
toward that very same thing that is the truest and
most pure, His Love. . . . Jesus's love.

Reflecting now I see that I am not . . . many things.
And that I can do most . . . nothings.
But that doesn't matter anymore.
Closing the book . . . I thought I would never embrace, I
realize now just how great He truly does taste.
And it was nothing I did . . . No seasoning of my concoc-
tion . . . Simply, it's Grace.

I am His and He is mine. Enough said.
Thank You, Oh Thank You, Lord . . . for it all. But simply
giving me this word, Hope . . . which started it all.
HOPE. What more do YOU need? That's who He really
is . . . He is Hope. He is Hope Indeed!

SOPHIA LUJAN

WISE IGNORANCE Confidence also empowers us to admit what we don't know, which gives us the freedom to learn. People who lack true confidence often cover it up by pretending to know everything. This rarely works, although the videos of such people doing stupid things usually make their way online where they brighten our days and make us all feel a little better about our life choices. When we are really confident, we can freely acknowledge where we still lack information or skill before we ski off a cliff, pilot a boat straight into a pier, or demonstrate to everyone that we lack the upper-body strength to hold on to that rope swing until we reach the water.

It's incredibly freeing to be able to say "I don't know" without feeling like you've disappointed the universe. It's also endearing. As we mentioned earlier, humility is attractive. People know that you don't know everything, and it's reassuring when you're honest about where your knowledge or experience has reached its limit. (It should be noted here that we are talking about not knowing something that is out of your expected knowledge base or experience. If you're the pilot of an airplane and your response to someone's question about how to land the thing is "I don't know," that's on you.)

Confidence gives us the freedom to learn, grow, and develop. It allows us to risk failure as part of that learning process, because we don't need to appear perfect to impress others or feel good about ourselves. As a result, we end up becoming and doing more than we ever could have if we had remained bound by the need to appear perfect.

CONFIDENCE GIVES US THE FREEDOM TO LEARN, GROW, AND DEVELOP.

As this confidence in who we are frees us to learn, we increasingly grow in our belief in what we can do. This confidence isn't based in arrogance or ignorance but in actual experience. We learn new skills, and we begin to see where we have talent and where we don't. We learn our limits and when to get help from others. This is a lifelong process, based on our own inner security in who we are in Christ. Secure always in God's love and the confidence that flows from it, we step into life and grow into who God has created us to be, finding the freedom we've always longed for.

I AM CONFIDENT, so I chase radical humility. In a world obsessed with status, I welcome humility. Does this make me insignificant? No. In fact, it's quite the opposite. It makes me teachable. It makes me capable. It makes me significant. And I use my significance—which cannot be shaken by position, season, or failure—for the purpose of service. Jesus—the greatest ever—modeled a new type of humility, humbling himself even to death on the cross. It's in his example that I find the courage to step into a supernatural confidence. I am confident, *so I chase radical humility.*

CREATIVE

DO YOU REMEMBER KINDERGARTEN, back when school consisted mostly of Play-Doh, games, and lunch? Chemistry textbooks and the quadratic equation were still in our distant and terrible future. A successful day was one in which we got a gold star on our drawing and didn't get in trouble for calling the kid beside us a poopyhead for taking our crayons.

Nostalgia may be coloring our view slightly here, but it does seem that one of the reasons most of us liked school more in those early years was that it was *fun*. And it was fun in large part because we spent considerable time drawing, coloring, building, and playing. In other words, we were allowed to be creative. "Every child is an artist. The problem is how to remain an artist once he grows up," said Pablo Picasso, the famous painter and sculptor who was one of the most influential artists of the twentieth century. He was right. What once was part of our everyday lives can fall to the wayside under the onslaught of daily assignments and to-do list items.

Creativity is not just the domain of children, however, even if we did eventually exchange our crayons for laptops and recess for study hall. Creativity is for all of us. God himself is creative—a fact made abundantly clear in the first chapters of the Bible. The Creator didn't follow a pattern when he made the world. He didn't take something existing and just get it to run better. He didn't copy someone else's idea. He started with nothing, added imagination and effort, and produced beauty. We are made in God's image; we, like him, are creative.

Creativity is the desire and ability to make something new, to develop something that doesn't exist, to express something that has not yet been spoken, to make connections that no one else sees, to solve problems that have no known solutions. We are creative in a thousand different ways, often without realizing it. And in this chapter, we want to celebrate it.

RESTORING HIS IMAGE We are made in God's image. We get to participate in the beauty and joy of creating. That has broad and wonderful implications for our lives. Before we look at what that means, though, we need to address some misconceptions about creativity, art, and the value of beauty that can get in our way.

You Have to Be a Good Artist to Create Art The first misconception is that creativity and artistry are only found in those special individuals who possess "artistic" skills. But creativity isn't just for artists and musicians, and artistry can be found in more than traditional art. For some of us, the last time we were proud of our creative abilities was when our mom hung our finger painting masterpiece on the refrigerator door. Once we got old enough to compare our creations with those of others, many of us decided we'd be better off employing our creativity in getting into and out of trouble than in improving our stick figure skills.

But expressing creativity in terms of writing or drawing or composing alone misses out on a world of beauty that God has for us, because we are all, in a sense, artisans. We all have a unique perspective of the world; each has a story to tell and a voice to use. In our own way, we can all understand and create beauty. Spend some time watching a bricklayer or stonemason work. If they love their craft and take pride in it, they aren't just building walls and fireplaces. They are creating works of art. Talk to an app developer about their current project. If you can get them

CREATIVITY ISN'T JUST FOR ARTISTS AND MUSICIANS.

to translate their terms into something resembling English, you will realize that creating an elegant, useful app is a fascinating blend of skills and creativity. It is art. An accountant developing a new Excel spreadsheet, an architect sketching blueprints, a barista making the perfect drink—creativity and artistry and beauty are found everywhere.

Creativity Doesn't Serve God The second misconception is that certain talents or jobs are inferior to others in the eyes of God. Subconsciously, many of us still feel that there is a hierarchy of holiness to vocations. Missionaries and pastors and such are up at the top. Everyone else is below them somewhere. Using our creative skills to make money or just to bring more beauty into this world is somehow considered inferior to doing spiritual things.

This sacred versus secular dichotomy is as pervasive as it is wrong. The Bible tells us to "use whatever gift you have received to serve others" (1 Pet. 4:10) and that whatever we do, we ought to do it with all our heart, "as working for the Lord" (Col. 3:23). When God told Moses to build a tabernacle, he told him to put a man named Bezalel in charge because God had filled him with his Spirit "to make artistic designs . . . and to engage in all kinds of crafts" (Exod. 31:1–5). God loves beauty! He invented the concept, and he loves to see us create. We are free to use our gifts to create, to develop, to produce, and to bless.

There is no higher calling than using our gifts to glorify God and to bless others. Creativity is one of the primary ways we do that,

THERE IS NO HIGHER CALLING THAN USING OUR GIFTS TO GLORIFY GOD AND TO BLESS OTHERS.

regardless of whether that creative ability is applied to crafting a sermon, writing a book, shooting a video, or building a house. All is sacred and beautiful as we use the gifts the Creator gave us to produce beauty and to bless others.

Beauty Isn't Important The third misconception is related to the second. This misconception is that beauty isn't particularly important. While we all appreciate beauty, often we think of it as optional, as icing on the cake, as a luxury that doesn't have a lot of value. To some extent this is logical. No matter how beautiful the car, if it lacks an engine, it's not particularly valuable. In our daily lives we need things that actually work, so we'll choose function over form if we have to make the choice. But that doesn't make beauty unimportant. There's a reason art has been part of every culture throughout history[1]: beauty—and the expression of it in creative ways—is part of who we are as humans. It is our expression of reality and of self.

We come by this naturally; we get it from our Father. Our love of beauty is one of the strongest evidences for intelligent design.

The almost physical need we all feel to stop and admire a jaw-dropping sunset would hardly have helped prehistoric man hunt dinner or evade enemies. It would, in fact, be a potentially deadly distraction. And biologists today still can't explain why the males of so many species use brilliant plumage, complicated dances, and creative mating calls to attract mates.[2] It's clear that females like it, but why? Shouldn't these flamboyant males have long since been devoured by predators and their less obvious brothers been the ones that survived? That's how natural selection is supposed to work. But even animals seem to love beauty. And so do we.

The truly amazing thing is, *we* are God's masterpiece. We are the art he proudly displays to the universe. To him, we are beautiful. And when we create beauty, we honor him.

CREATIVITY UNLEASHED If creativity is God's gift to us and a way we honor him, then we can and should embrace it. So what does it mean to be creative? What makes us curious? What enables

WE ARE THE ART HE PROUDLY DISPLAYS TO THE UNIVERSE.

creativity to flourish in our lives? Understanding its dynamics will allow us to use his gifts and to unleash his genius within us.

Creativity Is Curious Do you have kids (or cats)? Have you ever taken them to a friend's house for a visit? Within seconds, they probably began exploring—most likely to your chagrin as they soon started crawling into places your friend didn't expect to be explored. There is a reason for the old saying curiosity killed the cat. But curiosity also fuels creativity, ingenuity, and progress. The inquisitiveness and exploration that came naturally to us as children shouldn't be pushed aside by the pressures of adult life. It's healthy and fun and freeing to look at the world through the eyes of a child. Learn to be curious again.

Creativity Is Original While imitating others is a natural and effective technique to learn new skills or make quicker progress, it will only take us so far. God made us each unique, original, and uncopiable. We each have unique perspectives and experiences; we each have original contributions to make to this world. Don't be afraid to set aside the blueprints that others have created and dream something new. Don't be afraid to be a little wild, a little crazy, a little unrealistic. No one ever changed the world by excelling at being normal.

Creativity Is Innovative Most creations are actually built on or in some way related to existing creations. The ability to see connections between different things is a powerful and unique aspect of creativity. Innovation and development are creative acts.

Creativity Is a Process It's a journey, an adventure, an exploration of possibilities. That means failures and dead ends and radical rethinking are inevitable. If at first you don't succeed, welcome to creativity. You are literally making things up as you go along, often without a clear idea of what your end goal even is. Don't expect the path there to be a straight line. Relax and embrace the process, setbacks and all. You never know which failure will turn out to be the hidden door that opens a new world of possibilities.

Creativity Is Bold It envisions a future that doesn't yet exist and that others don't see. This sometimes makes it disruptive to the status quo. So creativity needs to gently set aside the opinions of negative people in order to pursue that future. During the creative

IF AT FIRST YOU DON'T SUCCEED, WELCOME TO CREATIVITY.

But that prayer took me on a journey of learning what it means to be "unoffendable." My heart's desire was to walk with God, but I was hesitant because it required me to let go of offenses and trust in the One who prompts us to keep no record of wrongs. The journey was not easy. It was messy, the path ahead wasn't clear, and it meant dying to myself over and over again.

But God continued to meet me where I was and paved a path for me to step into his strength. I learned that the journey to becoming unoffendable isn't just about refusing to be hurt by critical words or hurtful actions but also about breaking the hold that an offense might already have on my heart. Sometimes offenses come that I am unprepared for and don't feel able to handle. In those moments, I learn to strengthen my spiritual muscles, remember my own value in God's eyes, and understand how to handle the offense in a way that reflects rather than withholds the love of Jesus.

When it comes to our creative talents and skills, I believe the same journey must be taken. Criticism, offense, and insults will come our way at times. The path through that is messy and scary, eliciting discomfort and displeasure. But I believe it's a path that never ceases to welcome hope and joy. At times we might slip, trip, and fall, but God is still faithful. We are still valuable in his eyes. As we begin to understand that value, and all that he did to save us, we will become less affected by the minuscule things in life that don't give God glory and more inclined toward the things of life that do. We will become unoffendable.

IRIS MAMBA

process, when you are struggling to envision, explain, and create something new, others won't understand. This rarely stops them from giving you advice. Creativity that succeeds requires the ability to filter out the negative comments and focus on the vision. This isn't to say that input—even critical input—from others is always bad. Wise creators are willing to listen to others. But it's amazing how many people seem to feel their chief role in the creative process is to stand beside you and explain why what you are trying to do won't work. Remember, it's easy to criticize but hard to create. Don't be afraid to pursue creative approaches to the projects and problems you face, regardless of the opinions of those who don't yet see what you see.

FREE TO BE YOU No one will ever be as successful at being you as you. You're a unique creation, a masterpiece that cannot be copied. God used his limitless creativity in designing you because that's exactly what he wanted. In this competitive and insecure world, it's easy to look around and compare ourselves to others. We start to mimic someone else because they seem to be successful or happy, they seem to have what we want, or at least what we think we are supposed to want. We start to wish we were more like them and less like us.

But that line of thinking doesn't bring honor to God or life to your soul. Denying or downplaying who you are and trying to morph into someone you were never made to be is as ludicrous as deciding that because horses are beautiful, or because someone you admire really likes them, you will become one yourself. You can try to act like one all you want, but it's not going to work out well. Neither your wishes nor others' expectations should frame who you are. You are meant to be free to be you.

Of course, we all have areas that are still less than perfect—insecurities, immaturities, and weaknesses that the Holy Spirit is helping us work on as we grow in Christ. Freedom to be ourselves doesn't mean freedom to be a self-centered slob. But often, we go to the other extreme. We become so painfully aware of our perceived flaws and mistakes that we condemn ourselves for our failures, see only our faults, and decide that we deserve to be rejected. We are a failed experiment, a trial version that didn't pass the test, a mess not worth saving.

God sees us very differently. He doesn't ignore sin, of course. He does call us to holiness and to growth in maturity. But that process

NEITHER YOUR WISHES NOR OTHERS' EXPECTATIONS SHOULD FRAME WHO YOU ARE.

is never to make us into someone else. It's to help us be who we really are. It's not rejection; it's restoration.

In 2014, while disposing of their mother's estate, three brothers in New Jersey found a small painting in the basement that appeared to be a fake Rembrandt. Tiny, with a flaking surface, cracks in the back, and a frame that was clearly from an era two hundred years after the famous painter lived, the painting was "remarkably unremarkable," according to the appraiser. He valued it between $250 and $800. But during the auction, a couple of sharp-eyed bidders realized that it might actually be a missing Rembrandt, part of a series the painter had done when he was only eighteen years old. The bidding war that ensued ended with the unimpressive painting selling for over one million dollars. Conservationists discovered that it was indeed a genuine Rembrandt painting, although the artist's signature had been covered by a layer of varnish. The painting was eventually sold for over three million dollars and, after being restored and reunited with the other paintings in the series, is on display in the J. Paul Getty Museum in Los Angeles.[3]

Like that painting, our own beauty and worth may be partially obscured. Others may undervalue us, and we may agree with their estimate. But God sees our true worth. God can see beneath the dust and the cracks and our own poor attempts at "fixing" ourselves. He sees the priceless painting that he paid to redeem. He takes the time to restore us. And he doesn't regret it for a moment. We are priceless in God's sight.

You are free to be yourself. Free to grow. Free to fail. Free to learn. Free to love and free to be loved. Free to embrace the adventure that is life and the beauty of creation. Free to create. That is your birthright and your destiny.

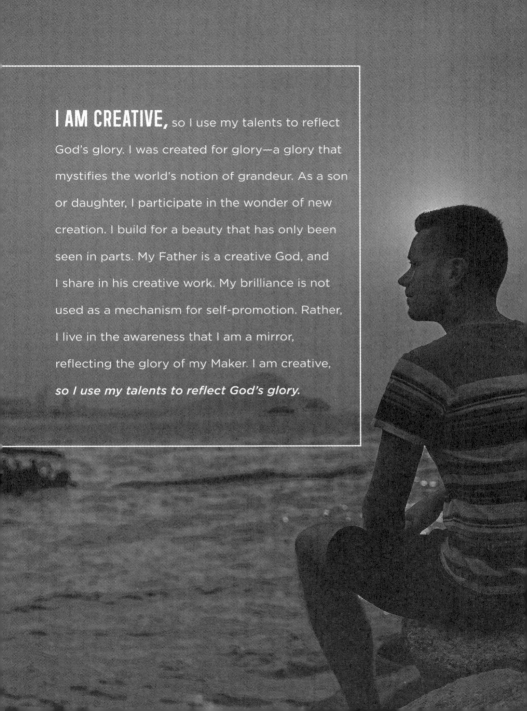

I AM CREATIVE, so I use my talents to reflect God's glory. I was created for glory—a glory that mystifies the world's notion of grandeur. As a son or daughter, I participate in the wonder of new creation. I build for a beauty that has only been seen in parts. My Father is a creative God, and I share in his creative work. My brilliance is not used as a mechanism for self-promotion. Rather, I live in the awareness that I am a mirror, reflecting the glory of my Maker. I am creative, *so I use my talents to reflect God's glory.*

CALLED

HAVE YOU EVER BEEN IN A CROWDED SPACE and noticed someone you didn't recognize waving at you from across the room? They seemed intent on communicating something to you, but you couldn't tell what they were saying. You tentatively waved back, you tried to motion that you couldn't understand them, you strained your brain in an attempt to remember who the person was—but it was no use. It was an awkward few seconds.

Then it occurred to you that maybe they weren't gesturing at you at all. So you turned around, and sure enough, just behind you another stranger was fully engaged in a pantomime conversation with the first person. Awkward just became humiliating. You discreetly lowered your hand, hoping no one noticed that you thought you were being called when you weren't.

Contrast that with the feeling of being chosen by name for a particular role or task. Maybe you were recognized publicly at school or you were given a promotion at work or you were asked to fulfill a new role in your church. Someone realized that your particular skill set and experience were exactly what was needed. They knew you had something to contribute, and they sought you out.

Whether you've experienced either (or both) of the above scenarios, it's not hard to see the difference. In one, you felt anonymous, ignored, forgotten; in the other, you felt unique and chosen. In one, you were overlooked; in the other, you were called.

Called. It's a powerful concept, one that implies so much.

You have something to offer.

Your contribution is recognized.

People depend on you.

You are known.

You are needed.

You are chosen.

You are sought out.

You have responsibility.

You have influence.

You have a mission.

It's probably safe to say that every human being would prefer to be called over overlooked. Something within us yearns for mission and for purpose. We want to be part of something bigger than us.

Think about superhero movies. No matter what movie franchise or mythical universe you look at, sooner or later, many of the heroes end up banding together to fight as a team. Individual heroes have their respective origin stories, of course, but eventually they work together to defeat the latest and greatest epic foe. These alliances usually have a certain level of dysfunction, which is played for laughs or drama or both, but the appeal of the superhero team is the mix of weaknesses and strengths that each hero brings to the team.

Those movies resonate with us personally because, while we have our share of weaknesses, we also know we have strengths, abilities, and gifts that the world needs. We may not be able to fly or turn into a massive green rage monster, but we have something to offer.

God agrees. And that is where calling comes in. The Bible presents God as personal, active, and involved in our lives. He didn't throw the universe together and then go on permanent vacation, leaving us alone to figure things out. He is watching us, guiding us, and helping us. He is *calling* us.

SOMETHING WITHIN US YEARNS FOR MISSION AND FOR PURPOSE.

That message is woven through the Bible from start to finish. King David wrote: "All the days ordained for me were written in your book before one of them came to be" (Ps. 139:16). The apostle Paul said, "For we are God's handiwork, created in Christ Jesus to do good works, which God prepared in advance for us to do" (Eph. 2:10). In another passage, he wrote, "For it is God who works in you to will and to act in order to fulfill his good purpose" (Phil. 2:13).

The Bible describes this concept in many ways:

Calling (1 Pet. 3:9)

Gift (Rom. 12:6)

Grace (Eph. 4:7)

Function (Rom. 12:4–6)

Plans (Jer. 29:11)

Choice (Eph. 1:4)

Appointment (John 15:16)

Sending (Isa. 6:8)

Consecration (Jer. 1:4–10)

These passages, and many others like them, show that God doesn't just love you, he also calls you. He has a specific future in mind for you to fulfill. Even if you feel as if life has overlooked you, God hasn't! He has a calling and a future for you. He isn't looking over your head at the guy behind you—he's looking at *you* and he's calling your name.

It's the journey of a lifetime to discover what this looks like for you. Your calling is unique because you are unique, and what God has in store for you will fit you like no one else. You get to spend the rest of your life walking and talking with Jesus—learning who he is, who you are, and how you fit into God's plan for this world. And that's the great adventure.

GETTING IT RIGHT Before we talk about some ways you can discover your calling, though, we need to clear up a few misconceptions that may be tripping you up.

Your Calling Doesn't Determine Your Value to God You don't have to earn your worth or win the right to be given a purpose. You're already priceless to God. He calls you to be his son or his daughter, not because he needs your help but because he loves you. And he gives you a purpose for existence, not because you earned it but because he willed it. You aren't an employee, working hard

YOUR CALLING IS UNIQUE BECAUSE YOU ARE UNIQUE.

to justify your paycheck or earn that coveted promotion. You're a child of the living God, learning to help out in the family business. You don't have to fear being downsized, overlooked, or let go if you don't measure up. Your place is secure, and you have the freedom to explore and grow into the skills and abilities that fit you best.

Your Calling Doesn't Remove Your Freedom to Make Choices God's will isn't a tightrope along which you teeter, trying to avoid the wrong choices on either side that will lead to immediate catastrophe. In most areas of life, God gives you great freedom to choose your path. If God had wanted a robotic servant, he could have built you that way. If he had wanted you guided only by animal instinct, he could have done that. But God made you in his image, with the ability to make real choices that have real consequences. God's sovereignty and power are not so fragile that he must remove your freedom to protect his plans. Instead, he is able to work in and through your choices, working all things together for good and guiding you into the future he has created for you.

Your Calling Isn't as Fragile as You Might Imagine Think about some of the heroes of the Bible who were anything but heroic at times. Abraham lied multiple times to protect himself and then slept with his wife's servant to try to produce an heir. Joseph bragged to his brothers and father about the dreams he'd been given, humiliating

US IS SPECIAL AND WORTH EVERYTHING TO HIM! WE ARE ALL HIS SONS AND DAUGHTERS, AND EACH ONE OF US IS SPECIAL AND WORTH EVERYTHING TO HIM! WE ARE ALL HIS SONS AND DAUGHTERS, AND EACH ONE OF US IS SPECIAL AND WORTH EVERYTHING TO HIM! WE ARE ALL HIS SONS AND DAUGHTERS, AND EACH ONE OF US IS SPECIAL AND WORTH EVERYTHING TO HIM! WE ARE ALL HIS SONS AND DAUGHTERS, AND EACH ONE OF US IS SPECIAL AND WORTH EVERYTHING TO HIM! WE ARE ALL HIS SONS AND DAUGHTERS, AND EACH ONE OF US IS SPECIAL AND WORTH EVERYTHING TO HIM! WE ARE ALL HIS SONS AND DAUGHTERS, AND EACH ONE OF US IS SPECIAL AND WORTH EVERYTHING TO HIM! WE ARE ALL HIS SONS AND DAUGHTERS, AND EACH ONE OF US

I LOVE THE STORY ABOUT THE SHEPHERD LEAVING THE NINETY-NINE SHEEP TO SEARCH FOR THE LOST ONE AND HOW GOD IS THAT WAY WITH US, BUT I'D NEVER APPLIED IT ANY OTHER WAY UNTIL RECENTLY.

I signed up to be a Sons & Daughters Ambassador, planning to start a small group with the students at my university. Then COVID-19 happened. The students were all sent home, and suddenly the entire population base for my planned group was gone. I thought my plan would fail and decided not to go ahead.

Twenty minutes after I decided to quit, I got a private message from someone who said they'd still be interested in joining my group. But it seemed ridiculous to have a "group" with only one other person in it. To be honest, I felt insignificant and my pride was wounded.

Then God spoke to me, challenging me to put my heart into it, even if it was just one person. My attitude began to change, and a fire ignited inside me to do the group— even for the one. I asked the Sons & Daughters team if I should go ahead, even with just one member, and they responded instantly with, "Yes, of course!"

That same day God actually brought in another person to join the group, someone I had not even thought of

US IS SPECIAL AND WORTH EVERYTHING TO HIM! WE ARE ALL HIS SONS AND DAUGHTERS, AND EACH ONE OF US IS SPECIAL AND WORTH EVERYTHING TO HIM! WE ARE ALL HIS SONS AND DAUGHTERS, AND EACH ONE OF US IS SPECIAL AND WORTH EVERYTHING TO HIM! WE ARE ALL HIS SONS AND DAUGHTERS, AND EACH ONE OF US IS SPECIAL AND WORTH EVERYTHING TO HIM! WE ARE ALL HIS SONS AND DAUGHTERS, AND EACH ONE OF US IS SPECIAL AND WORTH EVERYTHING TO HIM! WE ARE ALL HIS SONS AND DAUGHTERS, AND EACH ONE OF US IS SPECIAL AND WORTH EVERYTHING TO HIM! WE ARE ALL HIS SONS AND DAUGHTERS, AND EACH ONE OF US IS SPECIAL AND WORTH EVERYTHING TO HIM! WE ARE ALL HIS SONS AND DAUGHTERS, AND E *asking. I realized that I had closed myself off to people God wanted to reach through this group due to my tunnel vision and attempts to build the group on my own. God then put another person on my heart, and when I asked them, they were happy to join the group as well.*

Now we are in a really nice, strong, fun group. God has been ministering to us like crazy and has cultivated an environment of hungry, respectful people who just want more of God. We all open up to one another and are able to share cool things that God has revealed to each of us. Originally, I wasn't going to start the group, because I thought there needed to be all these people in order for there to be power and to make it worth it. But God reminded me that if He fights and cares even for the one, how much more should we. We are all His sons and daughters, and each one of us is special and worth everything to Him! So, do it even for the one. That's always enough in God's kingdom.

MIKAILA HOLDEN

and angering them. Peter denied Christ three times in a row and then fled when danger threatened. Thomas was so broken by grief and disillusionment that he initially refused to believe Jesus had risen from the dead. None of them managed to derail God's plan.

You haven't either. Yes, your choices have consequences, as we just mentioned. And yes, that can cause delays and problems and detours. But God uses even those to achieve his goals in you. This isn't an excuse to go out and disobey God, of course, but it does mean that even when you fail, God doesn't. When you make a mistake, God is still there for you. When your plans seem to have ended in disaster, he is getting ready to work a miracle.

Your Calling Isn't Just One Task, Vocation, or Achievement It can't be summed up in one word or phrase, like "I'm called to be a missionary" or "God wants me to be an artist," although it may include that. His calling for you is far more involved. It's multi-faceted, beautiful, and complex. It includes who you are, how you see yourself, the ways you grow, your personal relationship with him, how you relate to others, your influence on the people around you, your work and accomplishments, and countless other things. New aspects of his calling will become clear the longer you live, meaning the adventure is always fresh, always exciting, and always overwhelming enough to remind you to keep trusting your Father.

KNOCK, KNOCK Remember knock-knock jokes? Even told by a comedian, they are probably the lowest form of humor known to humankind. But if you have younger siblings or small children, you know that a knock-knock joke made up by a five-year-old who is still trying to figure out the concept of a punch line is pure agony.

> Knock, knock.
> Who's there?
> A cat.
> A cat who?
> Um . . . a cat . . . smells funny.
> [Hysterical laughter by the child.]
> [Forced laughter by everyone else.]

Eventually, thankfully, kids figure out what funny means. They realize that the person knocking at the door needs to somehow be connected to the last line of the joke. That still doesn't make the joke funny—it's a knock-knock joke, after all—but at least it's less painful.

Here's the point. When it comes to your calling, who is knocking at the door? And is that person connected to the bottom line of your existence? *Someone* has to be doing the calling, right? Someone is knocking at the door, and it's not the cat. You can't say, "I am called" without bringing up the question, "Who is calling me?" And yet, many of us do just that. We focus on the call and not on the one doing the calling.

So, again, who is calling you? *Jesus is*. Revelation 3:20 is often used as an evangelistic tool, but actually it was a quote from Jesus to people who believed in him: "Here I am! I stand at the door and knock. If anyone hears my voice and opens the door, I will come in and eat with that person, and they with me." It's the biblical predecessor to the knock-knock joke, only without the cringeworthy punch line.

Your calling doesn't start with what you want to do or with what someone else wants you to do or even with what God wants you to do. Your calling starts and ends with Jesus. Who Jesus is and what he has done are at the center of your life. You'll never be confident in your calling until you're confident in Jesus. At the end of the day, who Jesus is matters more than who you are, and what Jesus has done matters more than what you can do. When Jesus is the focus of your heart, your calling becomes sure and your future secure.

Far too often we make calling more about ourselves than anything else. In reality, it has *less* to do with us than anyone else. It starts with God, and it focuses on the people we will serve. We are just the go-between. Period. There is something very freeing about that realization.

So often we look to our calling for what only Jesus can provide:

Our *identity* cannot come from our calling—our identity comes from Jesus.

Our *value* cannot come from our calling—our value comes from Jesus.

Our *hope* cannot come from our calling—our hope comes from Jesus.

Our *security* cannot come from our calling—our security comes from Jesus.

Our *joy* cannot come from our calling—our joy comes from Jesus.

To Jesus, you'll never be more significant than you are now. You'll never be more worthy than you are now. You'll never be more accepted than you are now. And you'll never be more loved than you are now.

You need to let Jesus change your perspective. Stop striving to be worth more. Your calling or your accomplishments will never satisfy your need for significance, and they don't need to. Jesus does that. Just enjoy him, starting now, before you even know what he's called you to do. Let him open your eyes, heal your heart, and guarantee your future. Celebrate his reality and his presence. Focus on him, and things like mission and calling and vision and significance have a way of falling into place.

YOUR CALLING STARTS AND ENDS WITH JESUS.

Maybe you don't yet know what you are called to exactly. Your purpose in life may be shrouded in uncertainty, but you sense a desire to move toward it—whatever "it" is. If you hunger to know why God created you, listen for Jesus's voice. Learn to let him guide your life. Lean on him. Understand how he thinks.

WHAT IS YOUR CALLING? How do we do this? At the risk of sounding cliché, we get to know Jesus the same way millions of Christians before us have: through the Bible, through prayer, through worship, through meditation on God's truth, through observation and learning, through relationships, through listening to teaching and preaching, and so on. Those things were never meant to be empty spiritual rituals. They are life-giving ways of growing closer to Jesus.

Remember, the *who* behind the calling matters more than the calling itself ever could. What you do is incredible and valuable, but when your life is over, it will fade into the past. Your calling is for this lifetime, but you were created for eternity. Your relationship with Jesus will outlast what you're called to do in this age, and it deserves to be central in your mind and your heart.

So, with all of this in mind—that Jesus is the *why* and the *who* behind your calling—let's take a look at *what* your calling is.

Be before Do Who you are is always more important than what you do. Why? Because God isn't primarily looking for servants, but for sons and daughters who reflect his image. He's all-powerful. He doesn't really need your efforts on earth any more than a mother needs her three-year-old's help baking cookies. Chances are, adding a toddler to the baking process is going to create more chaos than cookies. But the time together, the skills the child learns, and the look of joy on his face when he eats a cookie baked "awl by himsewlf" bring joy to the mother's heart. God does give us tasks to do, but not because he's shorthanded. He wants to spend time with us, to teach us new things, and to delight with us in who we are becoming.

So, as you seek your calling and explore your future, focus first on being who God called you to be and on enjoying time spent with him, and you'll end up doing what God has called you to do. It's not always easy to focus on the "being" rather than just the "doing," because what you *do* is visible and tangible and measurable, while who you are *becoming* isn't. But it's worth it a thousand times over.

There's a big difference between *what you are* and *who you are*. The first speaks to seasonal identity (or identities); the second speaks to your core identity.

WHO YOU ARE IS ALWAYS MORE IMPORTANT THAN WHAT YOU DO.

YOUR UNIQUENESS IS A KEY TO YOUR CALLING.

What you are is largely fluid. Right now, you could be a student or developer or mother or entrepreneur or barista or golfer or some combination of all of these. Seasonal identities change over the years as you mature, develop skills, pursue professions, form new relationships, and take on new challenges.

But *who you are* will never change because it's grounded in the permanence of *whose you are*. You are a son or daughter of God. Period. And everything good and lasting in your life will find its hope and substance in that eternal truth.

Find What Fits God has called you to be and do certain things, and no one else can take your place. That means everything about you matters. Not just the good parts or the successes either. God has a way of taking the things we would call weaknesses or mistakes and weaving them into our future.

Your uniqueness is a key to your calling. You might have many alternatives in front of you, but some will be more natural, more fruitful, and more exciting to you than others. If God has called and prepared you for your future, then it makes sense that your interests and abilities could be clues to your calling. If you're wondering what direction to look for your future, ask yourself:

What am I good at?

What do I enjoy?

What do I have success at?

What opportunities are in front of me?

What can I do with the resources I have?

What do other people say I am good at?

What interests me or excites me?

What do I love doing with or for people?

What motivates me to action?

What comes naturally to me?

What do I feel drawn or compelled to do?

Your unique calling also means competition and comparison have no place in the kingdom of God. Trying to measure your value or success by looking at someone else is a trap. Paul wrote that people who "measure themselves by one another and compare themselves with one another . . . are without understanding" (2 Cor. 10:12 ESV). Each of us stands before God alone, and we receive our praise from him.

A Little Challenge Is a Good Thing The fact that your calling will likely be aligned with your interests and abilities doesn't mean everything will be easy. In fact, if there's not an element of impossibility to your dream, then you may not be dreaming big enough. After all, if you could do it on your own, then why would you need God?

OVER MY LIFE I CAN RECALL SPECIFIC MOMENTS— OFTEN DURING THE DARKEST TIMES, JUST BEFORE DAWN—WHEN THE LIGHT OF THE HOPE OF MY CALLING PERMEATED MY HEART.

The call did not look or sound like the dramatic calls I had read about in Scripture—there was no prophet's anointing, announcement, or declaration. Nor was there an immediate, bold, or obvious confirmation through awe-inspiring, supernatural means. It was a lot more subtle than that. At best, I can describe it as a knowing. I believed, but at times still struggled. Still the Lord persisted in whispers, kind and tender.

The process of hearing from Him and learning to understand that the call of my life is derived from the admonition to "love the Lord your God with all your heart, with all your soul, and with all your mind" (Matt. 22:37 HCSB) brought great freedom and joy in the process. I and the Lord can continue to work out my calling in time, through slow and steady practice. He is merely seeking those who are willing to humbly serve and boldly stand to see the kingdom of God come to earth.

RACHEL SLEDGE

Every hero recorded in the Bible is proof that God's calling will challenge you—just look at the giants, lions' dens, and fiery trials God's people faced. But without the battle there is no victory; without the fight there is no champion. God is calling you to face the impossible and defy it, not through your strength but his.

Following God's plan is hard. And it's also easy. That's one of the paradoxes of living for God. Difficulty and ease aren't mutually exclusive. Why? Because of grace. Grace is God's supernatural ability at work in us to do more than we could deserve or achieve on our own. When God's grace is on your life, things just work out. Maybe not immediately, and maybe not in the way you predicted, but ultimately they fall into place. You feel the wind at your back as you work. You find yourself enjoying many of the challenges. You face difficult situations, but you have the abilities you need to persevere.

WELCOME TO THE JOURNEY God's plans for your life are not a destination you arrive at, but rather a journey you take with him. There will be highlights and victories along the way as you navigate daily decisions to do your best, to follow God, to love people, and to use your gifts. If you are intimate with the moment, you *will* find greatness. You will find success, satisfaction, and purpose.

It's far too easy to forget to enjoy the present because we are fixated on the future: on the business we're going to start, on the book we're going to write, on the church we're going to plant, on

YOU ARE CHOSEN BY GOD.
YOU ARE COMMISSIONED BY JESUS.
YOU ARE NEEDED BY THE WORLD.

the family we're going to have. We think those things will bring us fulfillment, but they don't. They are wonderful, of course—but when we achieve them, we realize they are just waypoints, not the end of the journey.

The journey matters. Your calling is specific to you, but it's also wide and broad and multifaceted and continually unfolding. Yes, it includes the great things you will do. But it also includes things like discovering Jesus behind chance encounters, serving people at every opportunity, discovering joy and peace in your day-to-day life, overcoming obstacles with divine creativity, waiting and waiting and then waiting some more, learning new skills, walking through unexpected doors, and so much more.

You are chosen by God. You are commissioned by Jesus. You are needed by the world. Never doubt it again. *You are called.*

I AM CALLED, so I live each day with purpose. My life matters. Every day is energized with purpose. Each moment full of potential. God designed me on purpose, for a purpose, so I will not believe that my life is insignificant. Because of this, I invest in my character, calling, and community. I refuse to be stagnant, wasting away in self-pity. Purpose doesn't take a day off, so I won't be flippant with my time. I am called, *so I live each day with purpose.*

ONWARD

OUR VIEW OF OURSELVES is fundamental to how we live our lives. In fact, it's probably more important than our view on anything else in life, other than our understanding of God himself. Knowing who we really are—how God made us, how he sees us, who he created us to be, and what we are called to do—is crucial. It helps us make sense of much of the chaos that is life and hold fast to God's promises, even when we don't understand what is happening. It brings peace, stability, confidence, and a sense of purpose to our lives.

Maybe that's why it seems like the Enemy works overtime to get us to have a screwed-up view of ourselves. He understands what we often don't: when we really know who we *are*, we are unstoppable.

To sum up what we've seen in these pages, this is who we are, according to God:

I AM HOLY. Through Christ, I am restored to being fully human, reflecting the image of God in his awesomeness, his purpose, and his purity.

I AM RIGHTEOUS. God pardoned my sin. He wiped it out and declared me innocent of guilt and shame. I am part of the Father's family. As Creator and Judge, he defines righteousness. His word is final, and his word is, "You are righteous." No accuser in heaven, on earth, or in hell can refute that.

I AM LOVED. God didn't rescue me from sin because he felt some obligation. He didn't do it reluctantly or out of duty. He did it out of love. He loves me more than I'll ever understand, and he loved me before I had a clue he even existed. His love is eternal, unstoppable, and amazing.

I AM SECURE. I can rest safely even in the storms, knowing that the most powerful force in the universe is on my side. Nothing can separate me from God's love, and no one can steal me from his arms.

I AM CONFIDENT. I know who I am. I don't have to compare or compete with others to build an identity. I am created to be me, and I am beautiful. I am free to be bold, strong, humble, and gentle because I don't depend on the opinions of others to define me.

I AM CREATIVE. I am free to explore, free to build, free to fall and fail and fly. God has given me unique perspectives and gifts that I get to use to reflect his image as an artist in my own way.

I AM CALLED. God has a purpose for my life. My existence isn't random or senseless. God has called me for a reason. And while his purpose doesn't give me value, because I am already priceless in his eyes, it will bring glory to him and joy to me and many others.

BIGGER THAN YOU We've explored how these truths impact you personally. But it's never just about you. God didn't create you to live in isolation from others. Who he made you to be will only find full expression in the context of community. Yes, that is messy. But it's wonderful too. There is a broken, hurting world around you that needs what you have to give: your gifts, your talents, your passion, your experiences (even the painful ones). *You.*

You are God's work of art. But God doesn't paint in two dimensions. He didn't create you to hang passively on a wall and be admired. He created you in living, breathing, dynamic color—a masterpiece meant not only to reflect the Creator's perspective but to carry out his purposes. You are loved in heaven, but you are also needed on this earth.

Not only do others need you, but you need them. We are in this together. Throughout the Bible, God's people are viewed as a community. God called a human family in Abraham and Sarah; he rescued his people from Egypt; he chose the nation of Israel as his special treasure; he is building his church throughout the earth today. We are a spiritual family in Christ.

Our culture pushes a cult of individualism that promises freedom but brings only loneliness. But again, God "sets the lonely in families" (Ps. 68:6). We are part of a community greater than ourselves, and we are stronger together.

When the author of Hebrews told his fellow believers to avoid "giving up meeting together, as some are in the habit of doing, but [encourage] one another" (10:25), it wasn't because we somehow earn God's favor by going to church. It was because we *need* one another to truly live well.

"God will never give you more than you can handle" may make a cute meme, but it's bad theology, because it takes an individualistic approach to life's challenges. All of us go through times when we cannot handle the journey anymore—not alone anyway. That isn't because we've failed or God has abandoned us but because life wasn't meant to be faced alone in the first place. The community of faith is where we find help and where we help others.

ACCEPTING YOU Which of the seven "I Am" statements above is hardest for you to accept about yourself? Which of them triggers that doubting inner voice, whispering to you that it somehow doesn't apply to you?

We encourage you to dig deeper in that area or those areas. Pursue the truth for yourself until it becomes part of you. Don't

ME WITH INTRICACY. AFTER CRAFTING THE BRILLIANCE OF THE STARS, YOU FORMED ME WITH INTRICACY. AFTER CRAFTING THE BRILLIANCE OF
ME WITH INTRICACY. AFTER CRAFTING THE BRILLIANCE OF THE STARS, YOU FORMED ME WITH INTRICACY. AFTER CRAFTING THE BRILLIANCE
THE STARS, YOU FORMED ME WITH INTRICACY. AFTER CRAFTING THE BRILLIANCE OF THE STARS, YOU FORMED ME WITH INTRICACY. AFTER CRAF
NG THE BRILLIANCE OF THE STARS, YOU FORMED ME WITH INTRICACY. AFTER CRAFTING THE BRILLIANCE OF THE STARS, YOU FORMED ME WI
INTRICACY. AFTER CRAFTING THE BRILLIANCE OF THE STARS, YOU FORMED ME WITH INTRICACY. AFTER CRAFTING THE BRILLIANCE OF THE STA
THE BRILLIANCE OF THE STARS, YOU FORMED ME WITH INTRICACY. AFTER CRAFTING THE BRILLIANCE OF THE STA

DEAR FATHER,

I FEEL YOU IN THE WIND THAT BRUSHES AGAINST MY SKIN. I FEEL YOU IN THE WARMTH OF SUNBEAMS AS THEY REACH DOWN AND TOUCH ME.

I hear You in the melodies of the birds—each one chirps a song of cheerfulness.

They do not worry, so why should I? Your benevolent regard for me is endless.

Though chaos abounds in this darkened world, You remain steadfast and true.

When temptations arise and distort my view, You draw me close and strengthen me to press through.

You guide me through rough waters until I am dancing upon the waves.

You teach me to be still and know that You are God— the only One who saves.

I surrender my control as I wait on You, my Lord.

My spirit remains steady in the palm of Your vast hands.

Who am I to be so richly adored?
You graciously invite me to partake in Your grand plans.

After crafting the brilliance of the stars, You formed me with intricacy.
You gave me a name and loved me instantly.

I am awestruck by the wonder of Your Presence.
You are Creator, Righteous Judge, Deliverer, Father, and Friend.

I embrace the wind, soak in the sun's warmth.
I listen for Your whispers in the rustling of the leaves.
I will stand tall in Your strength like the sturdiest of trees,
And I will sing along to the birds' cheerful melodies!

My roots are growing deeper in Your love each day.
My heart craves to discover more of You—stay close, I pray.

CHRISTAL POTTER

just listen to what we have to say here. Dive into the truths of the Bible. It's easier today than ever in the history of humanity to study the Bible for yourself. Don't depend only on books (even this one) or sermons or podcasts. God wants to speak to you personally through his Word. You don't have to be a scholar—most of the writers of Scripture weren't! You just need to be willing to jump in, read, and listen to the voice of the Holy Spirit speaking to your heart through the Bible.

Embrace the journey. It's an adventure worth having, a life worth living, a story worth telling. Go for it. You've got this because God's got you.

ACKNOWLEDGMENTS

THIS PROJECT WAS AND CONTINUES to be a family effort, so there are some family members that we'd love to thank.

To our Father in heaven, thank you for calling us sons and daughters. By the power of your Spirit, may this book honor and represent your heart for your children and position us to follow in the footsteps of your Son, Jesus Christ.

To our brothers and sisters who shared their own stories, insights, and gifts, thank you for making this collective work possible. Together we are better.

To our parents, both by blood and by spirit, thank you for laying a foundation for us. Your faith, love, and trust make us believe that we can go further and occupy everything God has for us.

To our brothers and sisters at Revell, thank you for believing in the message and giving so much to make this book everything it could be. This wouldn't have happened without you!

To our sisters at the Fedd Agency, your presence and support along the way meant the world. Thank you for championing the message.

To the Sons & Daughters community and our Ambassadors across the globe, thank you for leading this world into the freedom, purpose, and adventure that God has placed within our hearts.

NOTES

I Am Holy

1. "H6918—qāḏaš—Strong's Hebrew Lexicon (KJV)," Blue Letter Bible, accessed March 17, 2021, https://www.blueletterbible.org/lang/lexicon/lexicon.cfm?t=kjv&strongs=h6918.

2. This term can be found throughout Scripture. See Exodus 19:6 and 1 Peter 2:9.

3. Addison Bevere, *Saints: Becoming More Than "Christians"* (Grand Rapids: Revell, 2020).

I Am Righteous

1. "G5486—charisma—Strong's Greek Lexicon (KJV)," Blue Letter Bible, accessed February 23, 2021, https://www.blueletterbible.org/lang/lexicon/lexicon.cfm?Strongs=g5486&t=kjv.

2. See Oxford Lexico, s.v. "shame," accessed January 26, 2021, https://www.lexico.com/en/definition/shame.

I Am Loved

1. C. S. Lewis, *The Four Loves* (New York: Harcourt, Brace, Jovanovich, 1960), 169–70.

I Am Secure

1. Saul McLeod, "Maslow's Hierarchy of Needs," Simply Psychology, December 29, 2020, https://www.simplypsychology.org/maslow.html#gsc.tab=0.

2. Jean M. Twenge, "The Age of Anxiety? Birth Cohort Change in Anxiety and Neuroticism, 1952–1993," *Journal of Personality and Social Psychology* 79, no. 6 (2000), https://www.apa.org/news/press/releases/2000/12/anxiety; Geoff Mcmaster, "Millennials and Gen Z Are More Anxious Than Previous Generations: Here's Why," University of Alberta, January 28, 2020, https://www.folio.ca/millennials-and-gen-z-are-more-anxious-than-previous-generations-heres-why/.

I Am Confident

1. Mark D. White, "Does Everyone Find Confidence Attractive?" *Psychology Today*, October 15, 2013, https://www.psychologytoday.com/us/blog/maybe-its-just-me/201310/does-everyone-find-confidence-attractive.

I Am Creative

1. For more on the cultural importance of art, see Susanne K. Langer, "The Cultural Importance of the Arts," *Journal of Aesthetic Education* 1, no. 1 (Spring 1996), https://doi.org/10.2307/3331349.

2. Ferris Jabr, "How Beauty Is Making Scientists Rethink Evolution," *New York Times*, January 9, 2019, https://www.nytimes.com/2019/01/09/magazine/beauty-evolution-animal.html.

3. Kirstin Fawcett, "6 Valuable Works of Art Discovered in People's Attics and Garages," Mental Floss, September 8, 2017, https://www.mentalfloss.com/article/504146/6-valuable-works-art-discovered-peoples-attics-and-garages.

SONS & DAUGHTERS is an initiative that helps young adults discover the adventure, freedom, and purpose found in their creator. Founded by the Beveres, what began in 2017 as a few YouTube videos for millennials has grown into a collection of studies, podcasts, events, and a global community with Ambassadors in over forty countries. For more information or to get involved, visit SonsAndDaughters.tv.

IF YOU'VE EVER WONDERED WHY YOU FEEL LIKE THERE'S MORE TO LIFE, THE ANSWER IS SIMPLE— THERE IS.

AMBASSADORS

IT'S TIME FOR US TO STEP INTO THE FULLNESS OF ALL WE WERE CREATED TO BE.

WWW.SONSANDDAUGHTERS.TV

 SonsAndDaughtersTV

 S&D

 SonsAndDaughtersTV

Introducing

MessengerX

Now you can access our entire
library of discipleship content!
Download the app at no cost today.

Scan the QR code to download MessengerX

MessengerX.com

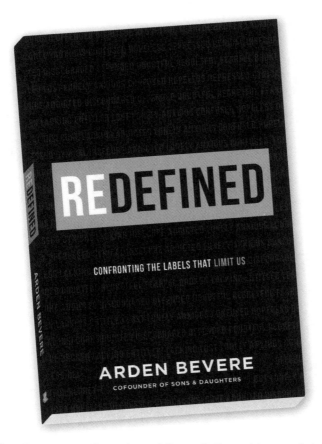

Discover Who God Created You to Be

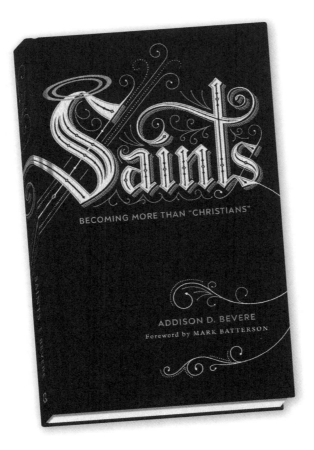

Addison Bevere shares what it means to be the people of God and helps us discover the fullness of the life God designed us for so we can reveal his faith, hope, and love to the world.